GHOST TOWNS OF FLORIDA

By

JAMES R. WARNKE

GHOST TOWNS OF FLORIDA
First Printing . . . April 1971
Second Printing . . . August 1971
Third Printing . . . November 1971
Fourth Printing . . . March 1972
Fifth Printing . . . June 1978

SIDE ROADS OF FLORIDA

First Printing . . . March 1973
Second Printing . . . June 1978

Published By
Roving Photographers & Assoc., Inc.
Box 1408
Boynton Beach, FL.
33435

Library of Congress Catalog Number 78-600554

Printed in the United States of America by Futura Printing, Inc., Boynton Beach, Florida.

ACKNOWLEDGEMENTS

Without the help of the following Floridians we would have found it impossible to compile the research material necessary for this book. We are deeply grateful to them.

Gordon Warnke of Boynton Beach
Robert Goble of Copeland
Homer Cato of Micco
George Hughes of Vero Beach
Charlton Thebeau of Miami
The Micklers of Chuluota
Warren Shroeder of Tavares
Yvonne Coggin of Ft. Pierce
Vernon Lamme of Boynton Beach
Lawrence Will of Belle Glade
Ron Ziegler of Deland
Dr. J. Manson Valentine of Miami
Elizabeth Smith, Crawfordville

TABLE OF CONTENTS

INTRODUCTION

They came to the promised land of Florida in the early 1800's for many reasons ... the consumptive for his health, the pioneer for a new home for his family, the merchant for a new start, the tycoon to enrich his holdings and the worker to lead a new life in the land of everlasting summer. Many found their yearnings satisfied, for here was a whole state that gave hope and a new beginning to thousands of settlers a hundred and fifty years ago, just as it does to millions of people today.

Farms and homesteads grew with the years and became towns and cities. Most of the new settlements in the tropical wilderness survived to grow with the state and are the cities we know today. Other budding towns were born with the hope and fever of the pioneers, but they languished on the vine of progress and became the subject of this book ... the ghost towns of Florida.

The term "ghost town" usually brings to mind a vision of old false-front clapboard buildings with loose doors swinging in the hot wind and tumbleweeds rolling along the wooden sidewalks of long ago. The town would perhaps be recorded in some obscure passage in a history book as the city of the future, due to a nearby bonanza of gold or silver. Maybe a grizzled hermit lives out his final years in the remnants of the saloon and regales his visitors with embellished tales of yesteryear. This is the romantic version of the ghost town of the Old West, but ghost towns in Florida?

The transplanted northerner, who is the average citizen of Florida today, would probably scoff at the notion that ghost towns could possible exist in his modern peninsula of golf courses, fancy restaurants and high rise apartments. Where in the whole state could such places exist? The reminders of the past are there for those who will pause and find them. To be sure, the old weatherbeaten buildings of the western type of ghost town no longer remain in the glittering facade of Florida today. Or do they? Come along with us and find them! Some of the historical villages **do** have the old hermit in residence. Some still **do** have the weatherbeaten clapboard structures remaining after years of forest fires and hurricanes. On other sites one can still find the hand made bricks and the old bottles of another era to remind him that he is standing on the soil of history.

How could a whole town composed of hotels, homes, post office and stores vanish so that today one is hard put even to find the spot where the village existed? The reasons are varied, but are usually due to hard economics. A bad freeze, a railroad bypassing the town or perhaps the local main industry closing its doors. Whatever the reason, Florida is dotted with those historical and little-known ghost towns that contributed so much to the progress of the state.

Researching old maps and courthouse records is the best way to find where the towns existed, but here we must be careful before we can label a site as a ghost town. Forgotten villages seem to fall into one of three categories. First, there is the true ghost town that once flourished with many buildings and residents and finally died with hardly a trace to show where it stood. Second, there are those towns that were once large and prosperous and have dwindled over the years to a shadow of their former selves, but **still have a few people living there.** In all fairness to these residents we do not wish to insult their village with the appellation of "ghost town"! Last, there are many sites that were named and are on the maps, but **never existed** as towns. Most of these are railroad stops for water and firewood and were named because the trainmen had to call them **something,** although a town never actually existed on the spot. We are primarily interested in the first category because there history was made and they are the most interesting sites of all.

Let us explore these sites and try to preserve a little of the almost forgotten history of the early towns. The encroaching bulldozers from our modern cities may soon destroy all evidence of our pioneer heritage. We believe we have a duty to preserve the past as well as to build for the future.

Roving Photographers, Inc.
Delray Beach, Fl.

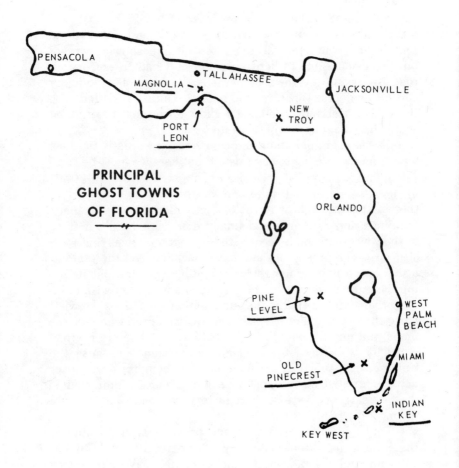

Chapter I

FOR THE WANT
OF A RAILROAD . . .

MAGNOLIA

Palmetto thickets and thorny wild blackberry bushes now cover the ground. The sweetness of jasmine hovers in the air and only the lonely cry of a jay bird breaks the silence of the piney woods. One walks along the weedy trails in search of the remains of Magnolia, but the town is gone. Oh, there are remnants, to be sure. An occasional hand made brick, a piece or two of sun-purpled glass or perhaps the shards of a flower-decorated chamber pot can be scuffed to the surface of the pine needles that cover the forest floor . . . not much else. However, if one looks closely enough, a further tangible reminder of the past can be found in the bushes. The Magnolia cemetery.

The old graveyard is known to but a few pioneer residents of the area today. It is remembered because some of the descendants of those who lie buried there still live in Wakulla County and are proud they were fathered by the early pioneers who dared settle in the Florida wilderness of the early 1800's. The early ones had dreams of carving a new life in the forests and scrub of north Florida and a few did live and prosper to realize that dream. Many found frustration and disappointment, for this new land did not give a good life without tremendous outpourings of labor and generous portions of good luck. The headstones in the vine-covered graveyard are hardly readable after one hundred and forty years, but, if one looks very closely, he can make out the names of Hamlin and Ladd . . .

In June of 1827, just six years after Spain ceded Florida to the United States, John, George, Nathaniel and Weld Hamlin came to the new land from Maine and founded the town of Magnolia. They chose a site on the St. Marks River a few miles north of the budding town of St. Marks to establish a cotton shipping industry and sell lots to others from the North who might want to take root in the new Utopia. They hacked out roads, built a steamship dock, erected a warehouse and placed ads in the northern papers much like the real estate hucksters

On a cold February morning, the mists hang heavily over the woods at Magnolia.

of today. The Kennebec Journal of Augusta, Maine, carried
the following ad on Sept. 22, 1827:

"It is every way eligible as a commercial depot and
place of business, it's site sufficiently elevated, dry and
healthy, combining every advantage which this part of the
territory admits. (Florida was not to become a state for another eighteen years.) Apalachy or St. Marks bay is the
only harbour which Florida affords in the Gulf of Mexico
where ships drawing over 6 feet of water find safe an-
chorage and ready access to the interior of the county by
road, from Apalachicola Bay to Tampa Bay, including a
seacoast of 350 miles in extant. Vessels drawing 8 feet of
water have no difficulty in ascending the St. Marks River,
13 miles, to the town of Magnolia. The tides ebb and flow
twice every twenty four hours, from two to six feet, varied
by the wind in this respect, differing singularly from the
other ports in the Gulf, which are little affected by the
tides, and only once in twenty four hours. Three good and
sufficient buoys have been placed on the banks at the entrance of the harbour, by order of the general government, and a lighthouse may be confidently expected
in the spring."

A huge rush of new settlers did not appear as a result of
the above broadside, however a few did take a chance on the
new land so far south of chilly Maine. Jason Knapen bought
the first lot on Broad St. in 1828 for $50. Others followed
suit and by the end of that year the first issue of the Magnolia
Advertiser was published (the seventh newspaper to be printed
in the Florida territory). Sample prices seem too good to be true
today, until one realizes that a "good strong shouldered
worker" only earned fifty cents for a 12 hour day — cornmeal,
80¢ a bushel; whiskey, 35¢ a gallon; poultry, $2.25 a dozen; and
ham at 18¢ a pound.
Cotton was the big crop and soon a rivalry started between the port of St. Marks and the upstart community of Mag-

Graves in the Magnolia Graveyard have been cleared of weeds by those who remember.

A child's desecrated grave in the Magnolia Cemetery.

nolia. Shippers of cotton bales would call at both towns and bid for the right to carry the rich harvest to the mills of New England. The Hamlin brothers had the edge here, for their relatives owned a large mill in the state of Maine. The Ladd family had married into the Hamlin family and emigrated to Florida about 1829 and thereby assured the Hamlin brothers of a market for their cotton. The city of Tallahassee, only fifteen miles north of Magnolia, was a railroad terminus. The extension of the rails south to Magnolia and St. Marks was imperative if the area was to prosper and not have to depend on ocean going ships to get their goods to market. The records of the day also show that large imports of goods needed the railroad to carry them inland. In 1829, merchants were handling "brown and loaf sugar, Canary, Malaga and Claret wine, Bleached Osnaburg, Powder, Shot, Lead, Cordage, leans soap, Foolscap Sealing Wax and Scotch Snuff." A crude plank road extended to the thriving city of Tallahassee but a railroad was the ultimate answer.

In 1835, the Hamlins were worried by the news that a group of financiers in Tallahassee were building a railroad to St. Marks and planned to by-pass the town of Magnolia. The brothers were already beginning to feel the pinch of competition from St. Marks and this meant the end to their "city of the future" and all their holdings in land and buildings. In spite of various meetings with the owners of the railroad, it was decided that a direct line to St. Marks would be the most economically feasible route. Magnolia didn't recover from this blow and began to lose residents and business to it's archrival.

The rails finally pushed through the wilderness, but it wasn't quite the New York Central! Although the builders had promised to furnish a steam engine, the first cars were pulled by mules. Slaves went ahead of the train and held the loose ends of the rails together so the wheels wouldn't leave the track and dump the adventurous passengers into the mud. A French traveler in 1838, one Count de Castelnau, wrote the following in his memoirs:

Mrs. Elizabeth Smith of Crawfordville, the noted Historian of wakulla County, visits the Magnolia Cemetery.

"The railroad is certainly the worst that has been built in the entire world. The road, however, is useful, for without it's help it would be almost impossible to take a heavy load of cotton across the sand that covers the country to the south, into which the horses sink at every step. They have tried several times to put a locomotive on this railroad, but its construction is so poor that the plan has been admitted to be impossible. Two mules hitched to carts, or a kind of uncovered truck, and driven by black slaves make the trip in seven hours. At each end of the railroad is a fine building or depot. More over, instead of being astonished at the bad construction of this railroad, one is inclined on the other hand to admire the bold thought that inspired a project of such a sort in a country inhabited by hostile savages and through almost impassible forests, which, so few years ago were not even explored by the whites."

So far as the records indicate there were no more lots sold in the town of Magnolia after 1836. The Ladd and Call families moved out and settled a few miles south in the new city of Port Leon. The sheriff auctioned off what the Hamlins were still holding and many of the buildings were moved, either to St. Marks or Port Leon. The warehouses were empty, the stores were without customers and the hotel that advertised itself as the "best on the Gulf" was without guests. Magnolia never recovered. The Ladds and the Hamlins lie buried in the old cemetery and above them the winds sigh in the slash pines as a requiem to their dreams. It would have been a beautiful town, if only the railroad had come just a little farther east . . .

A very rare split rail fence made of Cypress and "liter" pine.

Chapter II

THE FURY
OF THE WINDS . . .

PORT LEON

In modern terminology, Port Leon was a "spin off" from
the town of Magnolia. Two years after the railroad bypassed Magnolia and went on to St. Marks, wooden pilings
were driven in the coastal marsh and the flimsy tracks
reached the townsite of Port Leon. A pioneer by the name of
Call laid out the town, sold lots and for the first time the
term "waterfront property" was used in north Florida. The location seemed to have more to offer the settlers than other towns
in the area for here they could be away from the mosquitoes of
the piney woods and build their homes on the beautiful Gulf of
Mexico. An ad in the Pensacola Gazette for Dec. 21, 1839
stated:

SALE OF LOTS IN PORT LEON

"On Monday, January 13, 1840, will be offered for
sale at auction a part of the lots in Port Leon. This town is
situated on Apolache Bay, about 3 miles by the river, below St. Marks. It is handsomely located in the most elevated site on the bay **and is beyond the influence of the
highest tides.**"

This ad was placed by the railroad to attract new people to
the coast and thereby make the new railhead profitable. The
first lot sold in Port Leon that was recorded in the Leon
County courthouse went to Samuel Reed of Tallahassee for
$5. The deed also stated that he had "water privileges
in front of it." By 1841, even Daniel Ladd had given up
on the town of Magnolia and had moved his family to the new
town to the south. The Hamlins followed suite in 1842. Property
values boomed and two lots were sold in May of 1842, for
the huge sum of $3,450. A yellow fever epidemic the
previous year had almost finished the port, but more people
came and purchased property and the town's future seemed
assured.

A religious revival was taking hold in most parts of the Territory of Florida at the time, but the effects certainly were not

PORT LEON

Port Leon, located three miles south of
St. Marks on Apalachee Bay, was founded
in 1838 and incorporated in 1841. It was
developed by and became the terminus of
the Tallahassee Railroad Company. It was
a prosperous port for a few years and
was the county seat of Wakulla County.
Completely destroyed by a hurricane and
tidal wave in September 1843, the town was
not rebuilt. The residents moved further
inland and established Newport.

F-72   FLORIDA BOARD OF PARKS AND HISTORIC MEMORIALS   1962

Marker erected by the Florida Board of Parks and
Memorials in 1962.

being felt in the Port Leon area. A sailor visiting the port in 1841 wrote to his cousin, Benjamin French in Boston and described what he saw. (The following excerpt is from Elizabeth F. Smith's book, A TALE OF THREE TOMBSTONES).

"The land is very low, marshy and covered with pine trees, the water is very shallow and the ships when they load have to be anchored about 18 miles from the town and 6 miles from the light which is almost as bad as being anchored off Cape Ann. In speaking of the place everyone calls it St. Marks but now the business is removed about three miles down the river to a place called Port Leon. Port Leon is a new town but the houses (about twenty in number) are about the meanest kind. . .

"The people. Oh my! The "ruff scuff" of civilization and as to law. . .they don't know what it means, for Law and Justice are not in their vocabularies. I was asked to drink about 500 times and when I refused they would turn and look at me as tho they were shot. One man told me that I was the only person in Port Leon that would not drink and that he had heard of Temperance folk and he wanted to see how they looked so he begged the liberty of staring me in the face for a half of an hour.

"There is no church in Port Leon and Sunday they spend in playing Billiards, Drinking, Swearing, Smoking, etc. We went up to Tallahassee the second day after we arrived on the railroad but did not get there until the cars had run off the track three times."

At this time the new village had a hotel, a tavern, a yearly fair and a newspaper, but it did not have what it needed the most. . .a jail and a church! Many of the merchants in the area were making fair sums of money and because there wasn't a bank within twenty miles, they buried or hid any surplus wherever they felt it might be safe. When the yellow fever epidemic swept the town, many people died before telling their

Spanish stone wall at Fort San Marcos De Apalachee near Port Leon.

relatives where the family cash was hidden, thus leaving the survivors without funds. Even today the modern residents in the area find some of the long-hidden caches of silver and gold coins.

In the spring of 1843, Leon County was divided, and the southern half became the new county of Wakulla. Port Leon petitioned the legislature for the right to be the county seat and this was readily agreed upon. The summer passed without official action, but on a warm evening in the middle of September, the whole question became academic. Port Leon was hit by a large and vicious hurricane, and the entire town was virtually wiped off the map. Every building was leveled and lumber from the warehouses and homes was found later at St. Marks, three miles inland. Water covered the town to a depth of 7 to 10 feet, and the railroad terminal and bridge were completely gone. Those who survived the storm unanimously agreed to abandon Port Leon as a townsite, and they established the village of Newport, just north of St. Marks. It was said at the time that God destroyed the wicked city of Port Leon because "He was sorely displeased at what He saw."

Today the outline of the streets can still be seen on the higher ground, and a few building bricks lie scattered in the salt marsh. The town of St. Marks has a historical marker with a brief story about Port Leon, and a few artifacts can be seen in the museum at Fort San Marcos De Apalachee State Park. Port Leon is now deserted and abandoned to the winds that destroyed another dream of the pioneer settlers.

Old bottles found on the site of Port Leon include en-
crusted wine bottles and one embossed "Aromatic
Schnapps."

Nature takes back her own at Port Leon.

Chapter III

A SUWANNEE RIVER

SAGA . . .

A SUWANNEE RIVER SAGA

The banks of the Suwannee River are steeped in history. No other river in the United States, except for the Mississippi, has played so great a part in the heritage of the American people. For decades the river was used for commerce, a water highway, and a gateway to the interior of pioneer Florida. Even though Stephen Foster never saw the stream he immortalized in song, he made it so famous that hardly a school child today does not know the lyrics of his wonderful tune. Many towns sprang up along the banks of the Suwannee, but curiously, not a single large city exists along the river's entire length, all the way from the Gulf of Mexico to its head waters at Billy's Lake in Georgia.

This is really the story of two ghost towns. Old Troy and New Troy were each an integral part of Lafayette County in the 1800's, and neither of them exist today. Old Troy, in the year 1860, could boast a one-story log courthouse, five stores, two doctors, a saloon and a post office with William F. Bynum as postmaster. During the Civil War (or should we as southerners, say, "the War of Northern Aggression"?), deserters raided the hamlet in 1865 and put the torch to every building in town. Rather than rebuild the town on the old site, the residents salvaged a few documents from the ruins of the courthouse and established New Troy a few miles down the river.

By 1870, New Troy was a thriving community. John N. Kremenger was postmaster, D. M. McAlpin was superintendent of schools and William Edwards was the sheriff. The new courthouse was a two-story frame building. People would come from all over the county to watch the court proceedings, which sometimes lasted as long as two weeks. Mail was carried by horse to the small towns in the vicinity, and supplies were delivered by steamers from the coastal seaports.

In the years between 1880 and 1890, the community grew with prosperity and, in the year 1891, could boast a Methodist and a Baptist church, warehouses, stores, boarding

Where the courthouse burned at New Troy.

An old bail wire type canning jar and a spring door hinge
found at New Troy.

Relics of a bygone era found in one afternoon while
exploring the site of New Troy.

Split rail hog pen survived many a fire at New Troy.

houses, sawmill, cotton gin, grist mill, courthouse and jail, blacksmith shop and many homes. Two newspapers, The Lafayette County Messenger and The Lafayette County Enterprise, were both published in New Troy and a ferry had been established to carry passengers and goods across the river to Branford on the east shore. The area was teeming with game and fish and northern sportsmen making the long journey to the New Troy area were well rewarded for their efforts, for here was a land of plenty.

On New Year's Eve at the close of 1892, the courthouse caught fire. No one knows how it started but many said drunken revelers did it as a prank. In any case the building burned to the ground. The county officers, for a lack of a meeting room, held the next commission meeting in the Methodist parsonage on Jan. 2, 1893. Mr. T. Cates was the chairman and the minutes of the previous meeting were dispensed with as "the safe was still too hot to be opened" (the clerk of the circuit court of Lafayette County can show the old documents that bear scorch marks of the courthouse fire).

At this time the residents of the county were campaigning to have the county seat moved to a different location. An election was held in February of 1893 and the vote for the new county seat showed 299 votes for Mayo, 244 votes for New Branford and only one vote for New Troy. After the election it was discovered that one or two of the men carrying the ballots to the temporary courthouse in New Troy might have become a little too enthusiastic about the outcome and may have moved a few of the X's to a new place on the handwritten ballots. Rather than fight a long court battle to prove this, the commissioners decided to recanvass the voters and, in effect, hold a new election. On the sixth of March, 1893, the new count and hopefully the correct one, gave Mayo 218 votes, New Branford 187, New Troy 1 and Old Town 1. The new official seat of Lafayette County was declared to be Mayo and still is today.

Removal of the county courthouse from New Troy somehow spelled the end for the community and folks started

A lonely shack awaits for its owner's return . . . (near New Troy).

to move away. Merchants felt the pinch of the loss of business and were forced to close their doors in favor of other and more profitable locations. As trade dwindled, more folks left and one by one the buildings were boarded up and offered for sale to anyone at any price. There were no buyers. New Troy was gripped with a miniature depression and finally was completely abandoned.

Descendants of the early settlers, the Severance and Hill families still live in the area, but the site of New Troy is completely deserted. Giant oak trees spread their limbs over the bricks of the foundations and the Suwannee River glides silently by the few remaining pilings of the steamer dock. Hand cut nails and broken pieces of chinaware stick up from the sand and once in awhile one finds a rusty horseshoe from the blacksmith shop.

There is little to show today that here once existed a thriving town of over 500 people.

The only road to New Troy.

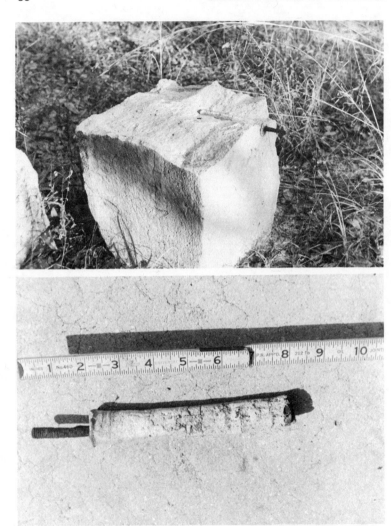

In the days before "store boughten" masonry anchors, holes were laboriously drilled into the stone, a bolt inserted and molten lead was poured into the hole to hold the bolt firmly in place.

Chapter IV

GREEN MONUMENTS
ON A ROCKY ISLE . . .

GREEN MONUMENTS ON ROCKY ISLE

The three hundred year history of Indian Key is made up of massacres, murders, shipwrecks and dictatorship. Perhaps no single piece of Florida real estate has absorbed more blood.

It all began in the late sixteen hundreds when some 400 Frenchmen were shipwrecked near the island and sought refuge there until they could be rescued by one of the rare ships that passed the key making north in the Gulf Stream.

The nearest white settlement of any size was St. Augustine, 400 miles to the north. The nearby keys of Upper and Lower Matecumbe were inhabited by savage bands of "Spanish Indians," who were offshoots of the northern Caloosa tribe and were known for their hatred of the white man. The Spanish had treated them roughly over the years and the warriors of the tribe would give no quarter to the hated Europeans. The end was not long in coming. Perhaps they saw the campfires of the survivors or observed them fishing for food during the day. The raid was quickly over. Not one of the ill-fated Frenchmen lived to return to his homeland, and when the Spanish later visited the scene of the massacre, they named the island "Mantanzas," or "place of murder."

The Indians had occupied the key for some time until the pirates drove them off and used it as a base for their operations against the Spanish ships bearing treasure from the mines of Peru and Mexico. The island offered a good harbor to the west and the buccaneers would pull over or careen their ships so that their masts could not be seen from the Atlantic side. When an unsuspecting ship would show her sail on the horizon, the pirates could quickly intercept the vessel, remove the bullion and sink the ship with no survivors. By the 1800's, the Navy had removed the pirate threat from the Caribbean, and the island slept.

As the nineteenth century dawned, a new breed of men had come to the Keys. The wreckers, they were called and the

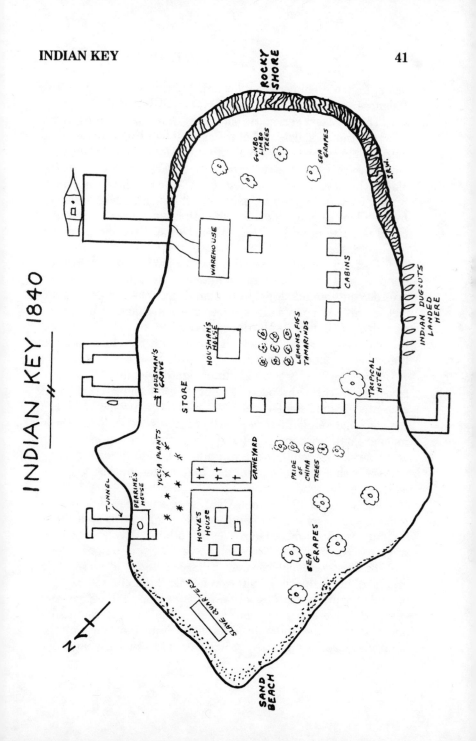

INDIAN KEY 1840

salvaging of shipwrecks became a large and lucrative business.

The wreckers served two purposes. They saved the lives of the unfortunate sailors and at the same time they salvaged what cargo could be brought ashore from the foundering ships. The courts were generous in awarding salvage claims and fast sloops and schooners owned by the wrecking companies waited for the cry, "wreck ashore!" These ships were manned by excellent seamen and the competition was keen to see who could put a man aboard the sinking vessel first and establish salvage rights.

Just east of Indian Key lies Hawk Channel, which forms a deep waterway running the length of the island chain and affords southbound ships protection due to the breakwater effect of the outer reefs. It is a treacherous channel; hundreds of ships have met their doom trying to navigate between the outer and inner ridges of coral that can tear out the bottom of the stoutest ship afloat.

There were only two aids to navigation along 150 miles of coastline — the lighthouse at Cape Florida and a small light ship at Carysfort Reef which was seldom on station. One can realize what dangers these early captains faced with these meager guides, when, even today, ships that are equipped with accurate charts, radio direction finders, Loran, gyrocompasses and are within view of hundreds of lights and buoys along the channel go aground.

Early in the 1830's, one Capt. Housman had established himself with a crew on Indian Key and quickly built up a thriving business on the misfortunes of others. His yearly take was in excess of $60,000 from wrecking operations alone and besides that, he owned a large store, a warehouse and had built the Tropical Hotel. The hotel in its heyday attracted many famous people traveling through the Keys and the guests were royally entertained. Fine wines, foodstuffs and clothing were there in abundance from the holds of the nearby stricken ships. (By 1850, over 500 ships a year were

A wall that up to a few years ago was still standing in the middle of Indian Key.

being lost on the coral reefs and the value of the hulls alone was estimated at over $16,000,000. The government finally erected a string of lighthouses along the Keys and set up refuge stations.) Housman was salvaging vessels from under the noses of the fleet at Key Largo and by taking his salvage to St. Augustine instead of Key West he would get 95% of the loss awarded to his company instead of the going rate of 50%. He accomplished this by bribery and payoffs to the judges and thereby earned the wrath of the other wrecking firms along the coast.

The other ship owners and the Monroe County authorities brought pressure to bear on Housman, but because of his friends in the Terrirorial government, he was able to have a new county created (Dade) and have Indian Key named as the county seat, thus thwarting those who wanted to see him in irons. In the new Dade County, he was the law.

Dr. Henry Perrine landed on Indian Key on Christmas Day, 1838. He was a famous botanist and had already contributed greatly to the science of horticulture. He had some new theories about growing various plants in the tropics and brought his family to Indian Key to experiment with varieties of sisal, oranges, tamarinds and fig trees. He was also a physician and treated the ailments of whites and Indians alike with the limited drugs of the day.

He and his family and the other 35 whites and 10 slaves living on the 11 acre island felt safe from Indian uprisings because the U.S. Navy has established a base on nearby Teatable Key and the government had assured them that there was absolutely no danger. Silas Fletcher had been appointed as postmaster in May of 1833. The hotel was prospering and there was talk of dredging a deep harbor so that the tiny isle could be established as an official port of entry on the southeast coast. The Indian threat was forgotten in the prosperity of the times.

Through the channel from IndianKey on the Gulf side, lies the highest island of all the keys, Lignum Vitae. Chekika,

Old survey marker on Indian Key.

The rocky south shore of Indian Key.

a famous Seminole war chief, hid a large band of his warriors there, well away from the prying eyes of the naval patrol boats. On the night of August 7th, 1840, he guided the Indian dugouts through the narrow waterway on the outgoing tide and quietly landed his force on the shore of Indian Key, just south of the Tropical Hotel. In spite of their careful approach in the darkness, the savages were spotted almost immediately and a settler's shot shattered the stillness of the hot summer night.

Terrible war cries echoed among the frame buildings as the sleep-dazed men groped for their weapons and tried vainly to defend their homes and families. Perrine herded his loved ones to safety under their house, where a tunnel led out beneath the sand to the dock. He stayed behind, because he felt that he could talk the Indians out of murdering the whites on the slim hope that he had been their friend in times of sickness and they had grown to respect the white medicine man. He stood on his porch and cried out for them to listen to reason. Perhaps the savages would have listened to his pleas, but by now they had broken into the liquor casks in Housman's warehouses and were crazed by drink.

They hacked Perrine to pieces and set fire to the settler's dwellings. Housman escaped by swimming with his wife along his dock, untying a rowboat and rowing to the naval ship MEDIUM anchored offshore. Perrine's family was nearly burned to death by the flames of the dock over their heads, but were saved by sailors who came to drive the Indians off the key. Chekika withdrew after killing almost everyone on the island and made his way to a hidden retreat in the Everglades, known as Chekika's Hammock.

The massacre at Indian Key created an uproar all over the United States, and the government was unable to explain how such a thing could have taken place under the very guns of the U.S. Navy. Black-bordered press dispatches demanded the legislators "take steps to revenge the dastardly deed and bring the Indians responsible to the hangman's noose." The

Empty cistern next to site of Housman's mansion.

Stone foundation of Perrine's house lies hidden in the bushes.

War Dept. realized that it had a blunder to correct and dispatched Lt. Col. Harney to the interior of the Everglades to find the Indians and deal out swift justice. Harney was an old hand at Indian warfare. Having fought Chekika before, he knew just about where to find the old chief.

The Everglades, between the coast and Chekika's Hammock, was dotted with the chickees and camps of the Seminole tribe, and so, to attract as little attention as possible, Harney had his men disguise themselves as Indians and then poled their dugouts slowly through the swamp to the main camp. Surprise was complete. Althought the soldiers had to approach the high ground across miles of open sawgrass, the Indians, in their disdain for the white forces, hadn't even posted guards or lookouts. Chekika was wounded in the first volley of fire and one Pvt. Hall ran him down, finished him with a knife and took his scalp. Only a few of the Indians were killed before they faded into the jungle, but Col. Harney's mission was complete with the death of Chekika.

Before returning to Fort Dallas (Miami), Harney hung the dead Indians from a pine tree as an example of the white man's revenge. Harney's foray into the wilderness of the Everglades broke the back of further Indian resistance and the savages realized that they were no longer safe from pursuit when they retreated into the swamps. The Second Seminole War drew to a fitful end in south Florida. Chekika's hair had been lifted and Perrine had been revenged. (The city of Perrine, just south of Miami, was named for the famous botanist).

Indian Key was never rebuilt. The settlers moved to other keys or made their way back north and nature took back the lonely island. Today the occasional visitor to the uninhabited key can make out the foundations of the house, hotel and cisterns. The sisal and fruit planted by Perrine over 130 years ago have taken over the remains and now grow in wild abandon — green monuments on a rocky isle. Along the shore can still be seen the fire-blackened stones of the Perrine home and all through the ruins are remnants of old bottles, clay pipes and broken dishes.

Capt. Housman, who later died in an accident at sea, lies buried somewhere on the east shore. He never had a chance, some say, to return and recover his hoard of money that he had kept kept hidden in a stone cavern somewhere close to his mansion. The key is deserted today and only visited by an occasional fisherman in search of hermit crabs for bait. Perhaps some day a historical marker will be erected across the channel at the wayside park on U.S. 1 to commemorate those who died on Indian Key, a part of the early history of Florida. In recent years the State of Florida has acquired rights to Indian Key and the island is "off-limits" to amateur explorers.

One of the last of the original homes at Pinelevel. Phosphate mines may soon take over this peaceful scene.

Chapter V

THE WILD,

WILD EAST . . .

THE WILD, WILD EAST...

Eight miles west of Arcadia lies the site of what once was the largest city in DeSoto County. Gray's map of 1886 shows Pinelevel as the only center of population for forty miles in any direction. The closest neighbors of any consequence were Myers (Ft. Myers) to the south, the hamlet of Sarasota to the west and the budding town of Manatee to the northwest.

Today a narrow 10 foot wide macadam road branches off from Highway 70, meanders through undergrowth, pine woods and farmlands and takes the rare visitor to an oak grove where once stood the courthouse of Manatee County. Except for an occasional red brick from the courthouse chimney and maybe a sun-purpled piece of window glass, there is nothing to show that this was once a roaring town, equal in wildness to Tombstone or Dodge City in the west of yesteryear.

Pinelevel was founded in the 1850's. The first settlers found a land teeming with game and fish and with fertile soil. The Seminole wars were at a standstill and the area was peaceful. Here, a man and his family could put down roots and raise children and crops in equal abundance. The area was as beautiful then as it is today — gigantic oaks draped with laces of Spanish moss, cypress knees as tall as a man's head, large stands of pine trees and several clear pools in Horse Creek that were right for "skinny dippin'" on hot summer days.

A weekly newspaper called THE PINE LEVEL TIMES was published by Edam Carlton, Esq. The village grew to become the center of all activity in the area and in 1866 the state legislature moved the county seat from Manatee over on the coast, to Pinelevel. At that time, Manatee County encompassed an area from the Caloosahatchee River to the south, to Tampa Bay on the north, and from the Gulf of Mexico eastward to the shores of Lake Okeechobee. It was a big land.

By 1880, Pinelevel could boast a courthouse, a jail, two churches, stores, warehouses, many homes and saloons. In the

Scattered bricks can still be seen on the courthouse site in Pinelevel

words of the late Charles Hagan, who was "raised up" on
the town's main street, "We had the wild west right here.
Tombstone, Abilene and Deadwood had nothing on us! We
probably had more blood spilled right here in Pinelevel
than in all the Seminole Wars combined..." The saloons
outnumbered the other businesses by 14 to 1 and as the town
was the only watering hole for many thirsty miles, Saturday
night was a riotous evening of gambling, drinking, shootings
and just plain "raisin' hell." Such an atmosphere was bound
to attract the outlaws of the day and the infamous
Sarasota Gang made Pinelevel its headquarters while they
raided banks and settlements along the Gulf. Twenty members
of the gang were finally captured, indicted and brought to trial
in 1855.

The courthouse was not finished at this time because of
lack of funds and the jail was so flimsy that it leaked prisoners
like a sieve. By "court day", only nine men were available
to stand before the bar of justice. They were charged with the
murder of the Sarasota postmaster, Charles E. Abbe, and one
Harrison "Tip" Riley. Because of various involvements of the
gang with the Florida Land and Improvement Co., the trial
had political overtones. Governor Bloxham had been giving
away land like it was going out of style and the two murdered
men were suspected informers of the land company and were
"taken for a ride" in the modern gangland fashion. It was
never very clear just why these men met their death, but it was
well known at the time that the Sarasota Gang did many
favors for men in high positions in return for living in compara-
tive immunity.

The trial was held in the summertime and attracted
newsmen from as far away as New York, Boston and Chicago.
There were no telegraph wires, of course, and their stories
were sent by oxcart to Tampa, fifty miles away. The mosquitoes
were out in full force, the accommodations were miserable
and the heat almost unbearable. An ox-drawn wagon train
bearing beer and whiskey from Tampa broke down on the

This sign points to a phantom of the past.

A farmer's lantern hidden in the pine needles.

rutted roads somewhere near Myakka which added to the woes of the arid members of the press.

All but two of the gang were acquitted. One of the guilty left the jailor a thank you note and vanished through a hole in the roof of the jail. The other had his sentence commuted to life but only served three years in jail. He died in Fort Myers about ten years ago, a respected and wealthy man. Much of the loot of the outlaws was was never found and the numerous sinkholes and small caves along the banks of Horse Creek may still contain money and jewelry.

In 1887, Manatee, Sarasota, and Palmetto banded together and had the legislature create a new Manatee County. Favored Manatee lost the election for the location of the new county seat and Braidentown (now Bradenton) was declared the winner by 39 votes. What was left of the old Manatee County became DeSoto County, and once again Pinelevel was the site of the county courthouse. Pinelevel's glory was short lived, however, for two years later, in 1889, the seat was moved to the new city of Arcadia over on the Pease (now Peace) River.* Pinelevel just couldn't compete with the new industries starting up along the riverfront in Arcadia and gradually declined to a lazy farming village. It all but disappeared in the ensuing years.

It is not quite time to say the final prayers over the site of Pinelevel. There are still about 40 farmers living in the immediate vicinity, but they too must soon depart. Phosphate industries are buying every available piece of land in what was once a thriving community. Those who want to stay on

---

* The Peace riverbed at Arcadia is one of the largest "boneyards" in the country. Huge bones of mastodon, tiger, bison and sharks can be found sticking out of the muddy shoreline. Visited by scientists from the Smithsonian in 1931, at the invitation of Mr. Vernon Lamme, State Archaeologist, the site yielded a virtual store house of prehistoric animal remains.

The "hanging tree" yielded to a hurricane several years ago.

realize that the encroaching industries may soon clear and strip the lands their forefathers homesteaded so many years ago. The old hanging tree still raises its huge limbs to the sky across from the courthouse site. Soon it may be wearing the heavy shroud of white dust of a phosphate mine. The survivors of Pinelevel (and we may well call them survivors) are unhappy with Arcadia's efforts to attract new industries, but they realize that there is little they can do to stop "progress" in the face of "all that there money-fixin' in Tallahassee." Pinelevel is still a beautiful place to visit. There is still plenty of game, the fish are abundant and there is peace. The land is still rich with crops and orange groves. If you want to see it, you had better hurry.

Chapter VI

OTHERS THAT HAVE
BEEN FORGOTTEN . . .

OTHERS THAT HAVE BEEN FORGOTTEN

Probably no one knows just how many deserted towns and villages there are in Florida. Surely, they must number in the hundreds. To research every hamlet that ever grew large enough to have a name would take a lifetime; however, there are many that did leave a scratch or two on the pages of history and this chapter will describe those which might be worthy of note. Some of these towns may still have a resident or two and to them I owe an apology for calling their places of residence "ghost towns"; however, they will probably be the first to admit that the town named "ain't what it used to be." Everything and every place must change over the years, but it is up to us, the living, to remember the heritage of our past. The towns mentioned in this chapter have earned a niche in history as a part of Florida's growing up as a state, and it is to them that we owe a debt.

Snake Bight. A fishing village that once existed at the turn of a century just east of Flamingo. The main industry was fishing for mullet and snapper for the north Florida markets, and the production of buttonwood charcoal. The town was noted for its disregard for the law and was the scene of numerous fights and murders. All that remains today are the rotted pilings of the main pier and a few "blob top" whiskey bottles to be found among the mangroves.

Elliot Key. Now called Islandia by the few people living there, Elliot's Key (as it was once called) was the home of several hundred early settlers. A main road traversed the island from north to south and the pioneers made their living by raising pineapples. A school was erected along with a church and a produce shed in the 1880's. A truck served as a school bus and its frame and engine can still be seen along the foundations of the school. The eastern shore is now used by Dade County as a park for boaters; how-

Rust and weeds take over abandoned farm machinery at Centralia.

ever, the interior is still in primitive state and many artifacts of the pioneers can be found.

Centralia. Located six miles north of Weekeewatchee Springs
on the west side of Highway 19 is the site of what was
one of the largest saw mill towns in Florida. The huge
mill operated from 1910 to 1921 and then closed after
exhausting the supply of local cypress timber. At that time
a passenger train made a daily round trip to Tampa along
with heavy trainloads of lumber for the waiting boats in
Tampa Bay. By 1930, most of the buildings had been torn
down or destroyed by fire. Remaining today are the foundations of the mill and depot, the railbed and several
dumps near the edge of the old town.

Cayo Pelau. Site of one of the earliest towns in the state, Cayo
Pelau is located in Charlotte Harbor and can only be reached by water. The history of this tiny island is replete with
Indians, pirates, smugglers and pioneer settlers. The Calu-
sa Indians built mounds here long before the coming of the
Spanish in the 1500's and their burial places are now being
investigated by archaeologists. On the south end of the island was Low Town, a pirate village in the 1700's, complete with a store, a blacksmith shop and several homes.
The remains of a shell road connecting the town with a
small shipyard on the north shore can still be seen, as well
as the rails used to bring boats out of the water. The visitor
today can find many artifacts of the early days, such as iron
kettles, bottles, buckles, ship spikes and dishes. The island
is now deserted.

Pinecrest. Six miles west of forty Mile Bend on the Tamiami
Trail on State Road 94 is the site of another early
settler's dream. Here was established a subdivision of
several thousand homes; lots were laid out, oil wells were
successfully drilled and a true city of the future

Remains of the sawmill foundation at Centralia.

began to take shape. The Great Depresson destroyed the
visions of the developers and the town died. The village
might have had a chance because of its location along the
original survey of the Tamiami Trail; however, Baron
Collier moved the path of the trail some miles to the north
and left Pinecrest served by a miserable dirt road. Al
Capone, in the 1930's built a large house in Pinecrest because the town was just over the Dade County line, in
Monroe County. The nearest law officers who served that
portion of Monroe County were located over a hundred
miles southeast in the keys and Pinecrest was, in fact,
lawless. It still is today. As late as 1967, Bill and Ethel
Hughes were wounded by passing hell-raisers while
standing in front of their gas station. The area has
known gator hunters, revolutionary military camps and
bootleggers. The foundation of Capone's house and other
buildings can be found in the scrub oaks along with the
trailers of modern day settlers.

Kitchings and Broadmoor. These sites are just west of the
present town of Roseland. Started in the 1800's nothing is
left to show where the towns existed. They are believed
to be on farms of present day ranchers and are inacces-
sible to the explorer.

Old Venus. Although there are still some people in residence,
the town, as such, has disappeared. The remains of a sawmill and filling station can be found, and there are many
deserted old houses in the vicinity. The site is located north
of Palmdale, about three miles west of Highway 27. The
boarded up post office still stands and the foundations of a
theatre and general store can be seen across the street.
The rusting hulks of two Model T's stand in the fields as
monuments of another year. Huge circular saw blades
stand abandoned against the hand-fed gas pumps of the
thirties. Old canning jars and whiskey jugs abound in the

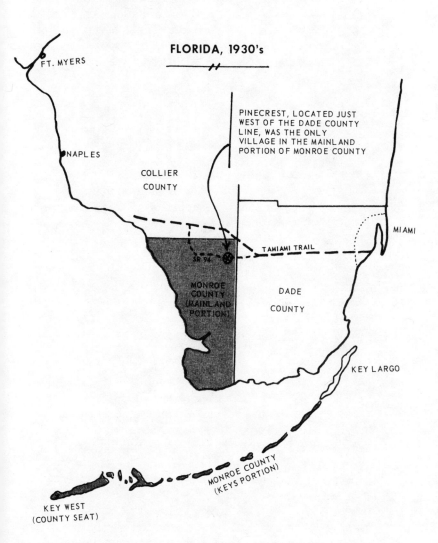

FLORIDA, 1930's

FT. MYERS

PINECREST, LOCATED JUST
WEST OF THE DADE COUNTY
LINE, WAS THE ONLY
VILLAGE IN THE MAINLAND
PORTION OF MONROE COUNTY

NAPLES

COLLIER
COUNTY

MIAMI

TAMIAMI TRAIL

SR 94

MONROE
COUNTY
(MAINLAND
PORTION)

DADE
COUNTY

KEY LARGO

MONROE COUNTY
(KEYS PORTION)

KEY WEST
(COUNTY SEAT)

Old time gas pump stands a lonely vigil near old Venus.

Early barn near Roseland. Home nearby has vanished.

remains of several old cabins that escaped the woods
fires over the years.

Johnstown. In 1782, this town overlooked the site of Ft. Caro-
line, just east of Jacksonville. Part of the area is now a
public park. The town had two taverns, one public house, a
livery stable, a dry goods store, warehouses, a hardware
store and a Masonic Lodge. At least 1500 people called
Johnstown their home in 1800. Present residents moving
into the area are finding the old foundations and are dig-
ging up many of the artifacts of bygone era.

Vareen. In Pasco County just east of Tarpon is the site of Vareen. Here stood a church, school and many homes of the
early settlers. The cemetery is the mute reminder that a
town existed here and only bushes and pine trees mark the
spot.

Punta Rassa. Just south of Ft. Myers is the townsite of Punta
Rassa. In the late 1800's it was the largest cattle
shipping center in the state of Florida. Hotels, restaurants, and saloons flourished and the town ranked with
Abilene, Kansas, as the center of beef commerce in 1894.
Here, too, was the terminus of the cable to Cuba and was
the first place in the United States to learn of the sinking of
the MAINE, which started the Spanish American War.
Punta Rassa was destroyed in the hurricane of 1873, but
recovered and was a boom town by the year 1900. It faded
during the thirties, but enjoyed a slight recovery during
the forties as the east end of the ferry to Sanibel Island.
The new bridge to Sanibel Island bypassed Punta Rassa.
There are some buildings remaining to reflect the glory of
the old village. Beams put together with wooden pegs, and
weatherbeaten clapboards, still intact after decades of
pounding by the elements, show that they just don't "build
'em like they used to." Back in the mangroves are the

Many homes were built off the ground to avoid frequent flooding in the rainy season.

reminders of the past — broken bottles, ox shoes and termite-ridden timbers of the old buildings.

Egmont Key. This semi-deserted isle guards the entrance to Tampa Bay and was a key strong point during the Civil War. The Spanish and the British fortified the key during their occupation of Florida and in 1898 the U.S. Army established Fort Dade on its rocky shores. Mostly deserted now, except for a small Coast Guard Station on the east end, Egmont Key is a fascinating place to explore. Miles of brick-paved streets overgrown with weeds, huge gun emplacements overlooking the Gulf of Mexico and dozens of walls and rooms of the barracks remain to intrigue the explorer. The British named the island for the Earl of Egmont, who was a land agent in Florida at the time. Egmont was the brother-in-law of Lord Hillsboro, for whom the Hillsboro River was named. The island is covered with artifacts of the past.

Belle Glade Area. Several small settlements such as Geerworth, Tantie, Gardenia and Fruitcrest were wiped out along with hundreds of residents by the terrible hurricane of 1928. All records were destroyed and very little can be found that tells of their history.

Wylly. This was a rip-roaring work camp back in the twenties, but the entire area is now a tree farm. Careful checking of the plow furrows will show remains of bottles, dishes, nails and hinges, but the site is very hard to find today. It was located on Highway 24, a few miles west of Otter Creek on the way to Cedar Key. A few old timers in the area can show you the general location.

Maytown. This village was once the half-way stop for travelers between Enterprise and Titusville. A railroad junction

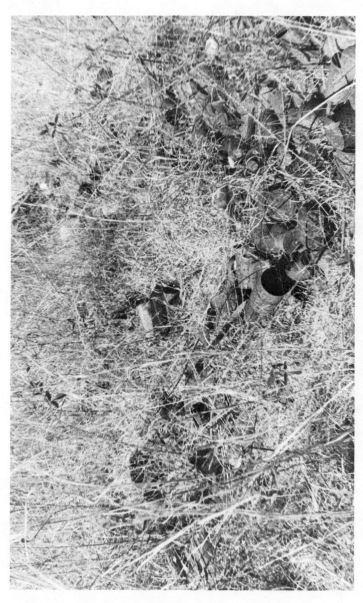

Trash dump at Wylly.

It's life work finished, a logging locomotive stands rusting on a siding near Wylly at Gulf Hammock.

The rails are silent near Maytown.

formed the nucleus of the small trading center. Although a
few people still live nearby, the area is dotted with deserted farms and houses and no longer exists as a thriving
community. It can be reached by a shellrock road leading west out of Oak Hill. Just follow the abandoned railbed . . .

Kismet. The town of Kismet was started by the Kismet Land
and Improvement Co. It lies just half a mile east of Lake
Dorr in the heart of what is now the Ocala National Forest. People from Ohio, Kentucky, Missouri, and
Virginia settled there and bought land for only $15 to $20
an acre. A post office was established in 1884 and the town
had a hotel, sawmill, tavern, school and many small but
comfortable homes. In the late 1800's there were plans to
extend a spur of the St. John's and Eustis Railroad to Kismet, but a hard freeze in the winter of 1889 froze
out the crops and spelled ruin for the young town. The
hotel was torn down and rebuilt on a new site near Altoona
and when the sawmill burned the next year, there wasn't
much reason for anyone to stay in Kismet. Those who did
stick it out for a few more years are now buried in a
forgotten graveyard overlooking Highway 445, three miles
to the north. The cemetery also contains the body of Duke
Alexander, the land baron for whom the nearby resort
area of Alexander Springs is named. Nothing remains of
Kismet today.

Conant. Although this site never achieved the full status of a
town, it is unique in that three lonely graves of its first
residents caused the State Highway Department to build a
sudden curve in Highway 441-27 so that the tiny cemetery would not be disturbed. Those who take the time today
to stop and ponder the headstones will find that they mark
the last resting places of Col. Richard William Singel-
tary 1837-1892, Mary Jane Singletary, 1845-1866, and

Flowing well and cistern near Maytown.

What pioneer family did this fireplace keep warm 75 years
ago? (Maytown area).

All that remains of Duke Alexander's mausoleum in Kismet cemetery.

Kismet graveyard.

The road to Kismet (Ocala National Forest).

Alice Keturah, 1855-1886. Conant was a big real estate development in the 1880's and was named for one of the backers of the Florida Southern Railway. It catered to the aristocrats of the day and a luxury hotel, private school and several expensive homes set the keynote. The developers soon found out that they couldn't make the subdivision hold its own by excluding the more common people and finally Conant dwindled to just a railroad platform and a small store. For a few years the remaining residents managed to keep their heads above water by raising and shipping watermelons, but they, too, finally left. An iron fence surrounding three gravestones is all that is left of Conant.

Sam Jones Old Town. The only reason we mention this site at all is that we are sure many people will say, "Why didn't you includes Sam Jones Old Town?" Many modern gas station maps still mark this site with the words "ruins," but their source of information is a mystery. Sam Jones was a tough Miccosukee war chief who at one time lived in the area. The supporting poles of his followers' chickees have been gone for over 110 years and the site never was a town any more than any other Indian village in the vastness of the Everglades. Sam Jones lived a long and colorful life (they say he was 110 years old when he died) and he fought against Col. Zachary Taylor in the Battle of Okeechobee on Christmas Day, 1837, but he certainly never established a town and there are no "ruins" to see. People have tried to find the site for years, only to get stuck in 'gator holes, run out of gas or wander fruitlessly through the swamp in search of a town that never existed.

West Tocoi. Here a small community thrived just before the turn of the century on the banks of the St. John's River. It, too, is listed on modern maps and is located about four

Foundation stones at Kismet.

Gravestone — Kismet Cemetery.

Under the ruins of this chicken coop was the rusted hulk of a Model T Ford.

miles north of Bostwick. West Tocoi was the terminus
of the Jacksonville, Tampa and Key West Railroad.
After a five hour trip from Jacksonville, steamers
would unload goods at the large dock at West Tocoi where
the merchandise would be taken by train to waiting markets in central Florida. The only trace the modern
travelers find today are a few dock polings rotting along
the edge of the river.

Ponceannah. Settled in 1858 by Rev. Lewis Ballard, Ponceannah grew to have a population of 150. it was located on
Blackwater Creek, 40 miles north of Orlando. The reason
the townsite was deserted is unknown and not even a
graveyard remains.

Seneca. Located 5 miles east of Eustis, Seneca had two
churches, a store, a saw and planing mill, two hotels
and over 600 acres of orange groves nearby. The site was
probably near what is now known as Indian Springs,
where an army payroll was buried to avoid its capture by
the Indians during the Seminole wars. Many deep sinkholes in the area have been dug by treasure hunters in
search of the missing gold.

Jernigan. This small hamlet was founded by a cattleman by the
name of Jernigan. Located 7 miles west of Kissimmee,
it never grew to any size and is incorrectly listed
in the history books as the early name of Orlando. Nothing
is left of the town in the rolling grove lands that cover the
site today. The ghost town of Shingle was located nearby,
but very little data on this town can be found.

Sylvan Lake. Founded by Johnson A. MacDonald in 1872, Sylvan Lake had two schools, a Presbyterian Church and a
population of over 200. The abandoned townsite is 2 miles
from the St. John's River and 7 miles west of Sanford.

Dry wood termites destroyed this dresser in an abandoned home near Ponceannah.

The old folks at home have long since been buried.

It is difficult to find an abandoned house that is free of vandalism.

Treasure hunters literally tore the walls off this house near Fort McCoy.

Traditionally, the builder put a coin under the hearthstone for good luck. Care to excavate?

What tales this gigantic oak could tell of happy days long past —.

House was deserted only 10 years ago — nature has taken over.

Peace River City. Settled on the Peace River about 1890, Peace
    River City, 5 miles north of present day Cleveland, was
    located in an area that is famous for pirate legends
    and buried treasure. Lettuce Lake, Punta Gorda and Char-
    lotte Harbor are nearby, not to mention that most famous
    of all spots in pirate lore, Gasparilla Island. The town
    never developed. A small subdivision has been started on
    part of the land, but the rest is still covered with
    underbrush and oak trees. Some historians contend that
    the pirate Gasparilla never existed, but was the figment of
    an early publicity agent's imagination to promote tourism
    for the old Charlotte and Northern Railway. Others say
    that the old bucanneer **did** live, led a murderous life and
    made his retreat and headquarters near the townsite of
    Peace River City at the upper end of Charlotte Har-
    bor. Whatever the truth, the region has been a Mecca for
    those afflicted with the fever of finding buried gold.

Acron. The settlement of Acron was located on the lower edge
    of the present Ocala National Forest on Acron Lake.
    Travelers reached the small town by paying a fare of $6.00
    for steamer passage from Jacksonville. After a 12 hour trip
    they disembarked at a small river landing 8 miles from
    Acron and finished their trip on a mule drawn wagon. The
    town was founded in 1875 by J. H. Cambell, Esq. Accord-
    ing to WEBB'S HISTORICAL AND BIOLOGICAL FLOR-
    IDA, ILLUSTRATED, published in 1885, "inducements to
    Immigrants are cheap homes, pleasant climate and school
    and church privileges". Although the town grew to a popu-
    lation of 300, it has disappeared from the map.

Extensive research has failed to uncover much about the
following towns. Some may have been just railway stops, others
were probably only a few houses and a store; however,

Deserted "tuppentine" workers cabin, Wakulla County.

at one time they did have names. They are included
here for those who might want to investigate further and
have the fun of learning more of Florida's history.

Floridale. Vanished in the 1920's. Location unknown.

Garden of Eden. On the east bank of the Appalachicola River
between Bristol and Chattachoochee.

Planter. Somewhere on the west shore of northern Key Largo.

Charlotta. North of Dunn's Creek on the St. John's River. Legend tells of the village being founded as a colony for peni-
tant prostitutes from England.

Keystone Park. An abandoned site 10 miles east of Tarpon
Springs.

Venables. East of Cedar Key, somewhere on present-day Highway 24.

Welshton. On Highway 464 between Ocala and Candler.

Survey. Somewhere near Bonita Springs.

Ocala Forest. Within the boundaries of the Forest are the sites
of several towns that were frozen out in the big freezes
of the late 1800's. Some of the names were Summit,
Bryanville, Syracuse, Churchill, Kerr City, Barronswood
and Messina.

Saulsville. Three miles north of Osteen in Volusia County.

Wiscon and Rural. Somewhere southeast of Brooksville.

Finally there is a graveyard and townsite without a name at
the Oklawaha Bridge just east of Sharpe's Ferry.

This was once a home near Welshton.

Near the ghost town of Welshton.

The telephone pole is an anachronism next to the Civil War period cabin. (Near Saulsville.)

Abandoned near Wiscon.

One of the few remaining buiildings of West Tocoi.

Bob Goble, Florida Forest Ranger, examines a still sound window frame made of "heart of pine."

Steps to a forgotten past . . .

Civil War era chimney near West Tocoi.

Chapter VII

UPDATE . . .

UPDATE

Since the original "Ghost Towns" was researched and published in 1971 much more information has come to light on the old towns of Florida. Many readers have called and written with further interesting facts about Florida's early history regarding towns and villages that no longer are on the maps.

To check each and every story and legend we have received from the old timers and history buffs would require someone's lifetime of research. On the following pages we have added what we think are authentic notes and additions to our original delvings into the origin and demise of Florida's many ghost towns. Some of the sites mentioned in the original book may have, by this time, been over run with condominiums and developments for which our fair state has a penchant.

While browsing through the scrub oak and palmetto thickets in search of the old villages and habitations you may find remnants of the past...broken dishes, old and purpled bottles, hand made nails or perhaps a coin or two...let these shards of history remind you of our pioneer heritage.

It would be safe to say at this time that Florida has at least one hundred ghost town sites. We hope that this little known portion of our state's history will not be forgotten.

The following pages have updates on ghost towns already mentioned and new information on sites recently "discovered."

Early settlers coming to the Lake Okeechobee area in the middle 1800's populated the islands of Ritta, Torry and Observation. Schools, post offices and homes were built and the huge fishing industry was started. The islands are not inhabited today and most of the land is used to raise sugar cane and other crops. The foundation stones of the post office can be still be seen on the north shore of Kraemer island. Old timers tell of a hermit who lived on Ritta Island and died in 1913. His body was not found for two weeks. He was buried as he was found...in his bed and the headboard extended above the ground as his tombstone.

Bean City, on the south shore of Lake Okeechobee, was founded in 1913 by Arthur Wells of Daytona Beach. At that time Highway 27 was the only road to Miami. String beans were not known in New York in the winter season and when they were shipped from Bean City they brought $13 a hamper. The 1928 hurricane wiped out the crops and thousands died in that terrible storm. Bean City came back in two years and they said there were beans as far as you could see. In the 1960's State Road 80 by-passed the city and the village is only a ghost of it's former self. Sugar cane has replaced beans as the major crop and the few residents still living there will admit that Bean City is a modern ghost town.

Near Dunnellen on Tiger Lake was a settlement known as Parkersburg. The town was founded in 1886 but the great freeze of 1895 wiped out the orange groves. There is little left today except a few concrete foundations.

According to Elmer Christensen of Haines City there was a village of Sisco just north of Pomona Park on Hwy. 17. It was established in 1870 by a Rev. Main and his 7th Day Baptists from New England. The freeze of 1895 wiped out the farmers in Sisco as it did in many towns of central Florida. Descendants of Rev. Main still live on Sisco Road but the town is long gone.

Malcolm Wilkins of Canterbury, N.H. tells us that he visited the site of Planter. This town once thrived on the Atlantic side of Key Largo just north of Tavenier. It was a pineapple shipping center for ships sailing for Baltimore. The remains of the dock pilings are visible along the shore at low tide. The site is near the road to Harris Park and is mentioned on USC and GS chart number 1249.

There are several locations of trading posts and cabins in

Home In Sisco, Florida, 1931.

the area around Everglades City. Small communities were started but failed to grow and survive. The Shark, Harney and Barron Rivers all have a lurid and wild history due to large numbers of criminals, poachers and outlaws inhabiting the area during the last half of the 19th century. The modern treasure hunter searching for loot must put up with mosquitoes, heat, swamps, lack of water and a maze of passages. Many have entered the region and have never been heard of again.

Mrs. G. F. Machaby of Jacksonville informed us that there was once a boom town called St. John's Park near Gibsonton. Her relatives settled there and at that time travelers took the train from Jacksonville and then by boat to the town-site. The only remnants today are pilings of the docks on the river shore. The town was established in 1908 and died a few years later.

Across the Intracoastal Waterway from Vero Beach was a thriving community known as John's Island. It was a fishing town with many homes, a church and schoolhouse. Several years ago we found many artifacts of the early village . . . pieces of pottery, sun purpled glass and hand made nails. Coins found with metal detectors dated from the turn of the century. Today the entire area is an exclusive subdivision bearing the same name.

Welshton was established by Capt. John M. Welsh of Erie,

Postmarks and cancellations used at Welshton.

Pa., in 1884. He staked out the village on seven thousand acres of pine land between Ocala and Lake Weir and erected a three story, forty room hotel. 200 Italian immigrants were brought to Welshton in 1885 to farm subsistance crops but the soil proved to be too poor for good farming. Several citrus groves barely got a good start when they were wiped out by the 1895 freeze. A post office had been established the first year but it too closed in 1898 for lack of business and the office was moved to Candler, another village just south of Welshton.

Mrs. C. H. Crabtree of St. James City, Fl., tells us that the town of Survey mentioned earlier in this book was actually the original name of Bonita Springs. Many towns mentioned in early histories of Florida had changes of names and now are prominent cities. She also told us about two more ghost town sites. One was called Caloosa and was located on the north bank of the Caloosahatchie River across from the present day hamlet of Alva. The second town was called Tropic City and was established in the new Lee County in 1887. It was situated about two and two-thirds miles south of the fire tower on the road to Pine Island from Fort Myers.

Mr. Larry Flegle of Tampa contributed the following. "There was a place called Vandolah situated on the road that runs along the railroad tracks between Ona and Fort Green Springs. It was a sawmill town and when the mill burned down the town died. There is one house left today."

For cemetery buffs there is a historic graveyard started in the late 1830's to serve the now gone village of Shingle Creek. It is located on busy Hwy. 192 between Kissimmee and Disney World. Many pioneers of the area are buried in this old cemetery that is part of the Shingle Creek United Methodist Church. Although there was a large community there around the turn of the century, it is now a shady place of the past.

Ellaville was situated on the north bank of the Suwannee River near the Madison and Suwannee County lines. It was a station of the Jacksonville, Pensacola and Mobile Railroad, ninety five miles from Jacksonville and 70 miles from Tallahassee. There is a State Park on the south side of the river now, but for those who want to explore the woods, many foundations can still be found hidden in the surrounding forest.

Gardenia was referred to on page 72 of the original section of this book. Joann Crawford of Leesburg Public Library sent the following information. Fruitland Park was established in the late 1800's. The postal authorities refused to recognize the name Fruitland Park as there was already a Fruitland in the State and they feared that confusion would arise from Florida having two such similar names. At their request, the name of the budding town was changed to Gardenia in 1884. A railroad, put through the town just previous to that time, had listed the town as Fruitland Park in all their printed matter and refused to recognize the new name of Gardenia. Consequently, all freight and express had to be directed to Fruitland Park and all mail addressed to Gardenia. This caused a great deal of confusion which lasted from 1884 to 1888 when a petition was sent to the postal department to have the name changed to Fruitland Park again and this petition was granted in 1888. A civil engineer by the name of H. E. Campbell filed a survey of the area on Nov. 7, 1885.

Ethel City was founded a few miles north west of the intersection of Lake, Orange and Seminole counties in the 1800's. Today there are only a couple of cabin sites remaining. It was a stop on the Atlantic Coast Line railroad along with the nearby ghost town of Wekiva.

In 1886 a book was published by Sidney Lanier titled "Florida: It's Scenery, Climate and History." Because of the uproar in recent years concerning the cross-state barge canal and the destruction of the beautiful Oklawaha River, we think it would be interesting to quote from that pamphlet about the steamboat landings of the early days on one of Florida's last unspoiled rivers:

OKLAWAHA RIVER — Runs from the central part of Sumter county through Lake Harris and Griffin, generally northward across the northern portion of Sumter, the whole of Marion, and a part of Putnam counties and empties into the St. Johns opposite Welaka, 25 miles above Pilatka and 100 miles above Jacksonville. From it's mouth to Leesburg (which is usually spoken of as head of navigation, though the steamboats go a few miles further to Okahumpkee on Lake Harris) is about 170 miles. Silver Spring Run, which is the river formed by the outburst of Silver Spring is nine miles long and empties into the Oklawaha about a 100 miles above it's mouth. The run is navigable for the Oklawaha steamboats and at low water Silver Spring is the head of navigation on the Oklawaha for steamboats. At such times market-vegetables and farm-products from above, as well as supplies and general freights from below, are conveyed by barges between the Leesburg country and Silver Spring. The Oklawaha landings are as follows:
Distance from the mouth of the river:

Fort Brook	35 Miles
Iola	50 Miles
Eureka	60 Miles
Sandy Bluff	68 Miles
Palmetto Landing	78 Miles
Gores	83 Miles
Durisoe	89 Miles
Graham	94 Miles
Delk's Bluff	100 Miles

Silver Spring	109 Miles
Sharp's Ferry	114 Miles
Moss Bluff	140 Miles
Stark's Landing	155 Miles
Lake Griffin	160 Miles
Leesburg	170 Miles

Some of the places mentioned in the old book are prominent today, of course, but the others? Long gone.

Enterprise is an "almost" ghost town today. In 1841 the town was founded by Cornelius Taylor and the early pioneers built a grist mill, a saw mill and a steamboat to navigate the St. John's River. The budding city was really set into motion by the arrival of Jacob Brock in the mid 1850's. He built the Brock House, central Florida's first hotel, and constructed a large pier out into Lake Monroe for his steamers which ran to Jacksonville twice a week.

Grover Cleveland, Gen. Ulysses S. Grant and William Jennings Bryan came for vacations. Harriet Beecher Stowe wrote about Enterprise in northern travel articles and attracted tourists by the hundreds. Brock built a courthouse when Enterprise became the county seat of Mosquito County, which took in parts of Orange and several other present day counties surrounding the area.

As in the case of so many other towns in central Florida the freezes of the 1890's wiped out the citrus crops. When the railroads extended service to Sanford, the steamboats were no longer needed and ninety-five percent of the population of Enterprise were forced to locate elsewhere.

To see the interesting remains of this famous old steamboat town exit I-4 at the Enterprise-DeBary interchange just north of Orlando and then drive left to Enterprise.

Decaying pilings (left) are all that remain of the old Brock
pier at Enterprise — once a bustling St. Johns River port.
In its heyday, the pier (above right) served steamers such
as the Frederick DeBary which ran regularly between
Enterprise and Jacksonville, carrying cargo and passengers.

SIDE ROADS of FLORIDA

by
James R. Warnke

Photographed and Published
By
Roving Photographers and Associates, Inc.
Marion Bentley Wall   Roland James Dack
Box 1408
Boynton Beach, FL.
33435

Printed by

Futura Printing, Inc.

Boynton Beach, Florida
33435

FOREWORD

Millions come to Florida -- and never see it. They are like motorized pellets in a glamorized pinball machine, hitting the flashing lights of widely publicized artificial attractions before bouncing out of the state and back home.

Our beautiful natural springs, which might have been preserved as treasures of serenity, have been ballyhooed into carnivals with barkers in glassbottomed boats and exhibits of simpering underwater mermaids and performing seals.

Porpoise shows and reptile exhibits, alligator farms and deer parks, simulations of the African veldt with lions roaming at large, monkey and parrot jungles and water ski shows infest the state.

If that is "your thing," you can bounce from one to another on any of the main routes, visit all the commercial aquarium shows, see cobras milked and -- if you have anything left -- get milked yourself at a Miami Beach clip joint.

But the Florida we love , those of us that have lived here most of our lives, has no admission fee, except the desire to appreciate beauty, the awareness to see it and the time to enjoy it.

Our amazing shows are the wonders of ever-changing clouds, low to the land, sometimes like placid white cattle grazing down a blue pasture, often in tumultuous thunderheads that boil in majesty or in threatening black line squalls. We love to watch them trailing a skirt of rain across the saw grass swamps, cabbage palm hammocks and pine forests. If you came to Florida and didn't feel close to the clouds, you really didn't see Florida.

The real Florida is a land of beauty and serenity, a

place to take time to enjoy dawns and sunsets beyond the river against silhouetted pines. It is a place to hear the wind in the needles of the pines and to remember the dancing wraiths of Spanish moss on live oaks. Florida is for quiet contemplation on a sea beach, watching pelicans skimming the breakers in single file like long vanished pterodactyls.

Florida is for quiet fun, crabbing in the bays, catching shrimp from bridges and holding "shrimp boils" on the beach, catching whiting and yellow tail croaker in the surf and cooking them over a driftwood fire, going lobstering and clamming. It is for walking and seeing and doing and having fun.

Florida is for amazement, wonder and delight, and refreshment of the soul. It may take a little more time to hunt out and enjoy the real Florida, but you will be well repaid.

Take time to feel the cathedral stillness of the Corkscrew Swamp near Immokalee, where centuries old cypress will speak if you can hear. Take time to go deep into a South Florida hammock and see fragile wild orchids. Listen to the rustle of shells on the beach, see mullet leaping for the fun of life, watch the changing moods of rivers and lakes ruffled by changing winds.

Take time to see the night blooming cereus along the Indian River, century plants sending their seed stalks aspiring, the sea oats, the black eyed susans and "Candles of the Lord," those waxen-white yucca flowers on the dunes. Go out over the reefs in the Keys and look down through water clear as air at forests of living coral and sea plumes where jeweled fishes dart in and out of grottos.

Take the by-ways, drop into quiet little towns where neon does not yet hide the stars, visit the Suwanee and the upper St. Johns, cruise up the St. Lucie or Loxahatchee.

Be able to say: "We saw the real Florida."

From "My Florida" by Ernest Lyons, author, columnist and editor of the Stuart News

INTRODUCTION

The urge to get off the well-beaten path and explore the countryside has been an American tradition ever since motor-driven wheels replaced horses. Thousands of motorists give in to their adventurous instincts and find that side trips to out-of-the-way spots add zest to vacations and Sunday drives. Others would like to strike out on their own but hesitate because of possible wasted hours in barren areas or for the fear of getting lost or stuck on a remote country road.

The aim of this book is to guide modern day explorers to some of those places that would otherwise remain hidden, unknown and unseen. I have purposely avoided any mention of commercial attractions, State or Federal parks, historical sites or locations that charge admission. Hundreds of brochures at your motel desk describe every tourist attraction in the area and repeating the information here would be boring and pointless. Leaving the Interstate or Turnpike for sideroad exploring is richly rewarding and can turn a humdrum vacation into an exciting trip that will be long remembered.

Every county has something or some place that is unusual. Talk to people! Everyone is proud of the area he lives in and more than glad to tell of things that are not on the oil company map. Libraries are especially helpful as are members of the local historical society. if the town has a museum, you have a goldmine of information at your disposal. County highway maps are very detailed and can be bought at the local courthouse for about fifty cents. These maps show every side road, jeep trail and lane and, in most cases, houses, mines, lakes and streams. Ask your waitress, gas station attendant or motel clerk about things to see in the area. You will be pleasantly surprised!

I have listed many interesting spots and areas in this book that I have "discovered" in my wanderings around the Sunshine State, however there are hundreds more waiting if you will only leave the main roads and follow your nose. A great man once said, "He who is without curiosity is poor indeed."

Be "a shunpiker"!!

EAGLES NESTS AND SLAVES

The area north of Eustis in the central part of the state is known locally as the Big Scrub. Hundreds of square miles of high sand country covered with pine, scrub oak and palmetto await the traveler who yearns to see the real backwoods of Florida. Here is one of the last strongholds of the deer, panther and black bear. Hunting and fishing camps, trailer parks and roadside businesses are fast encroaching on this vast wilderness, although the National Forest Service is fighting to preserve what is left.

Drive north from Eustis on Hwy. 19 through Umatilla and Altoona and turn right on State Road 445. This side road cuts through an almost untouched section of the forest and therefore is a good location to get the 'feel' of the Big Scrub. About a mile after leaving Hwy. 19 look on your left for a high embankment crowned with two or three cedar trees. If you feel ambitious, climb the slope to see an old cemetery dating back to the 1880's. This was probably the graveyard of the long gone town of Kismet which once thrived about three miles to the south of the knoll. Here also is the tomb of Duke Alexander, for whom the nearby Alexander Springs was named. The tomb has been desecrated and only a few red bricks remain scattered in the weeds.

Leaving the cemetery, drive on for about five miles and take the first dirt road to your right just after you cross the Alexander Run bridge. Although many of the small trails and roads in the forest are sandy traps for the unwary driver, this one, known as Forest Service Road 52B, is no problem in good weather. Take your time and watch the woods closely. Deer are plentiful, birds abound and wild rasberries grow along the edge of the road. After about two miles watch for tall dead trees on the left about three hundred yards away. Bald eagles have built their nests here for years and some of the huge collection of

sticks they use for a home measure eight feet across. They
return to the same nests year after year and if you have
binoculars with you, you may be lucky enough to see the
huge birds feeding their young. There is a fork in the road
at this point so keep to your right.

The road continues on through thickets and woodlands
for about three more miles and ends at the river where
there is a small launching ramp if you wish to continue
your explorations by canoe. The water is not deep enough
at this point for larger boats. (For a fantastic trip some
time, canoe the Alexander Run from the springs all the
way to the St. John's River.) Here once stood the ruins of
a small Spanish hacienda on the shore of the river. Ex-
cursion boats from Alexander Springs once made the
ruins a stop so tourists could explore the old stone walls,
however nothing is left today.

Remember the fork in the road three miles back? If
you are feeling really woodsy, turn right on the way back
and follow this trail for about two and a half miles until it
dead ends in a small hollow known as Hinson Camp.
Watching for snakes, walk about sixty feet down a dim
trail to your right and you will come to a small lake on
your left. This lake was created by the excavation of a
huge indian mound that once stood here. The shells from
the mound were used to build the roads at the Springs
recreation area. On your right, under the tree roots you
can see the outcroppings of the original shell mound.
Many artifacts have been found here including pieces of
pottery, stone tools and spear points but the huge old
mound is mostly gone now due to modern man's
draglines.

Going back to SR 445 continue north to Astor Park.
Along the way you may see many pine trees in the forest
that still bear the hatchmarks of the turpentine workers.
The tapping of the trees has been stopped since this area
was made into a National Forest. Do you notice the big

The abandoned Kismet cemetery.

furrows dug through the woods at several places? These
are the fire breaks made by the forest service plows to
contain forest fires into a small area.

At Astor Park turn right on Hwy. 40, cross the St.
John's River and turn left on Hwy. 17 at Barberville.
Several miles north turn left on State Road 308 at
Crescent City and continue for eight miles to a T in-
tersection at Fruitland, where you turn left (south) on
State Road 309 for three miles to Georgetown. Here is the
ferry that you will take across the St. John's river to
Draton Island. If the ferry is on the other side of the
river, blink your lights for service but don't be in a rush.
People in these parts just aren't in a hurry for anything
and don't cater to those who are.

Eventually the ferryman will tell you to drive onto
the big barge and he will push you across the river with
his small outboard equipped boat. The barge will make a
good landing on the first try if the wind isn't blowing too
strong and you can drive off to enjoy the serenity of
Draton Island. The island was used for a slave trading
station before the Civil War. Part of the huge white
homestead on the south end of the island dates back to the
1830's. Several old homesites overgrown with weeds and
vines are hidden away in the backwoods and a few bricks
may still be found that were part of the foundation of a
hotel. This is all private land and Florida has rather strict
trespass laws, so be sure you have permission before
exploring off the main road. There isn't much to see on
Draton Island today, however the ferry trip over and the
restful drive past moss laden trees lets you enjoy an
afternoon trip that is hard to duplicate elsewhere.

After leaving the island, drive north on SR 309
towards Palatka where you will find several small
restaurants specializing in Florida foods...a fitting close
to a quiet and restful day.

Gravestone in the Kismet cemetery.

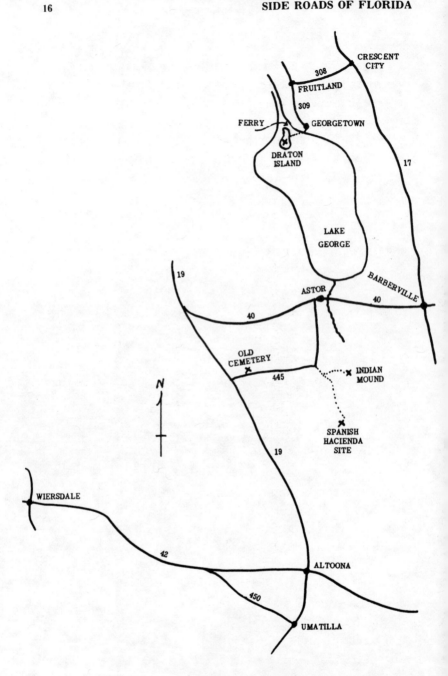

SITES DESCRIBED IN EAGLES NESTS AND SLAVES

78 MILES OF WILDERNESS

Thousands of motorists drive it without seeing it. Thousands more traverse its length without hearing it. They are in a hurry. They are trying to get from A to B in the fastest possible time and they curse what they mistakenly call a monotonous stretch of blacktop rimmed by nothing. The road wasn't created to be a scenic highway, merely a shorter way to get to Naples from the Gold Coast, but it does have rewards for those who will only stop and take the time to absorb the glory around them. Alligator Alley!

As you approach the toll gate at either end of the Alley you are warned that there is no fuel, service or food for the next 78 miles. It is probably the loneliest stretch of road in the eastern United States. It is also one of the finest areas in Florida to study the tremendous amount of wildlife in the Everglades and the Big Cypress swamp.

The most rewarding way to see what the Alley has to offer is to start out from Ft. Lauderdale just before dawn so that when the first tinges of the rising sun bloom in the east you will be in a good place to pull off the road, preferably near one of the many bridges about 20 miles west of Fort Lauderdale. If it is a weekday, there probably won't be another car in sight and you can hear and see the awakening wilderness completely surrounding you to the horizon and beyond.

The birds put on the biggest show. Egrets, ibis, curlew, ducks and dozens of other species all take to the air by the thousands. Looking to the horizon with binoculars you will see the glory of their wings over the waving sawgrass. Walk down below the bridge and along the canal bank and here you will perhaps see a great blue heron walking on stilt like legs in the shallows looking for his breakfast of minnows. If you startle him, he will fly softly away with a slow beat of his six foot wingspan.

Here also are the puddle ducks and the hundreds of coots
chortling incessantly as they bob their heads under the
water looking for tidbits. Walk carefully, as here is the
home of the water moccasin and he might be out looking
for a last frog before retiring for the day to his reed-
hidden home. This is also the domain of Florida's great
fighting fish, the large mouth bass. If you have a rod with
you, try a small surface lure along the edge of the rushes.
With the tableau of the unspoiled land around you and the
cries of the birdlife as a symphony you will enjoy fishing
at its finest!

The eastern half of the Alley cuts through the heart of
the vast Everglades. Hundreds of square miles of waving
six-foot-high sawgrass conceals the slowly moving water
making its way to the Gulf of Mexico. During drought
years, huge fires devastate the 'glades and the land lies
parched under the tropical sun. Most of the birds leave to
find wet areas in the National Park or the Corkscrew
swamp and the fish die by the millions. The important
role of the alligator in the balance of nature now becomes
evident. When a 'gator makes an area his home he digs
large holes in the muck to the limestone below and also
creates channels through the grass. When all else has
dried up, these holes and furrows become the last haven
for the remaining fish and turtles so that when the rains
begin anew the seeds are there to repopulate the waters.
The great swamp has managed to thrive for many
thousands of years without man's help and will continue
to do so if well-meaning but ill-advised man will only
leave it alone.

As you leave the halfway point heading west you will
see a rather abrupt change take place as the sawgrass
merges and then gives way to the forested area known as
the Big Cypress Swamp. At one time here grew the
largest cypress trees in the south but intensive logging
operations from 1930 to 1945 left few of the mighty giants

The roar of an airboat sometimes breaks the quiet solitude of the Big Cypress swamp.

for later generations. You can still see the huge stumps along the roads, and the overgrown logging trails are used today by the hunters. The oldtimers say that at one time they could show you bald cypress trees 150 feet high and seventeen feet in circumference. If you would like to see the area in more detail turn south on State Road 840 before you get to Hwy. 29. This is a gravel road that runs for about fourteen miles to U.S. 41 and goes through the heart of the backwoods. A small canal on the west side of the road is full of bass, garfish and mudfish and if you drive slowly through here at night you are almost sure to see deer, opossum and raccoons.

Developers are trying hard to 'modernize' the wilderness areas of south Florida. Let's hope they don't succeed . . .

A DRIVE INTO THE PAST

The southeast corner of Florida is not only largely undeveloped but is rich in the remnants of history of our state. Here Baron Collier used his millions to open the cypress swamps to developers and settlers. Here the mighty engineering drama of the Tamiami Trail unfolded. Here the farsighted conservationists carved out the boundaries of the Everglades National Park while the logging interests devastated the once virgin Big Cypress Swamp.

Starting at LaBelle turn south on SR 29 and drive through Felda, Immokalee and Sunniland. This is oil country. The walking beams of the oil wells dot the countryside to the west of the road as you pass through miles of pastureland with hundreds of grazing cattle. If it were not for the telltale palmetto trees you might think you were in Oklahoma.

You pass Alligator Alley at what the oil company maps call Miles City although there isn't a single habitation in sight. Continue on for thirteen miles to a small road leading west to the hamlet of Copeland and then turn north at the sign "Janes Memorial Highway". Highway it is not, but for ten miles you will be treated to the sights and sounds of the interior of the true cypress swamp. The road follows the old logging railroad grade and about every 600 feet you can see the dim outlines of the tram line cuts that brought the logs to the main line. Stop and enjoy the small ponds and canals that line the trail teeming with wildlife and marvel at the size of the tree stumps left by the loggers.

Drive south from Copeland on SR 29, cross Hwy. 41 and you will reach Everglades City. The canal on your left is salt water for now you are nearing the Gulf of Mexico. Everglades City is a quiet town, long famous for the great fishing to be had in the nearby Gulf. The Sportsmen's Club has attracted Presidents and notables from all over the world. The city is not anxious for the highrise beehives of progress to appear and still uses the lampposts of the twenties.

Just south of Everglades City the road makes a long sweeping curve around a placid bay to the fishing village of Chockoloskee. Alongside the calm waters are wayside stops with picnic tables, ideal for a lunch stop and maybe a little fishing (No license needed). Shore birds and waterfowl dot the sand flats in the bay as they search for seafood morsels.

The town of Chockoloskee is built on the huge shell mounds left by the early indians. Once isolated from the mainland until the new road was built, the village has long been a haven for those who found it to be the ideal location for a really restful vacation combined with some of the best fishing in the world. You will sense the change in tempo of life the minute you step from the car that brought you from a different world.

Smallwood's store was started in 1904 as an indian trading post and has changed very little in almost seventy years. The old coffee grinder, pots and pans and home remedies still adorn the shelves along with some modern supplies. Miss Thelma Smallwood is always glad to tell you of the history of the store and the surrounding village and will recount how a movie was made on her front porch. The old frame building has withstood many a hurricane and is a living relic of Florida's history.

Driving back to the north, turn left (west) on Hwy. 41 for sixteen miles to Collier Seminole State Park. Just inside the entrance to the park on the right hand side is the huge walking dredge that helped build the Tamiami Trail back in 1927. Operated by Meece Ellis and Earl Ivey, the dredge "walked" its way through the swamp on the material shoveled up by the gaping jaw in front. Plagued by swarms of mosquitoes and tropical heat the dredgemen worked 18 hours a day to complete what is now Hwy. 41. Millions of pounds of dynamite were used to blast the bedrock of limestone to build the roadbed above the swampwater and as an engineering feat ranks with the Panama Canal. Stop and wonder how many motorists using the trail today realize the amount of money, blood, sweat and tears that were expended for their benefit.

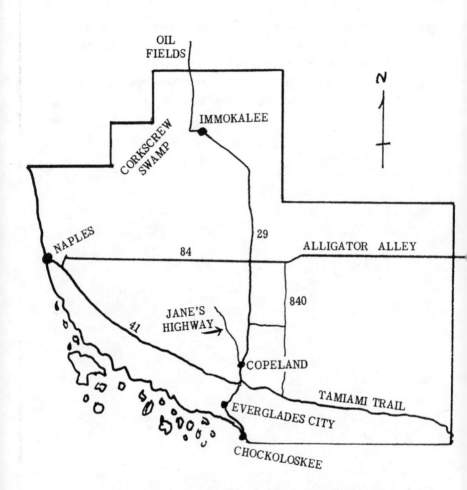

COLLIER COUNTY SHOWING CORKSCREW SWAMP, JANE'S
SCENIC DRIVE AND CHOCKOLOSKEE ISLAND

A BRIDGE TO NOWHERE

Did you ever have the urge to explore a tropical island? An island with the remains of old houses, relics of yesteryear, an ancient shipwreck and perhaps a hermit or two? Such an isle really exists within shooting distance of US 1 about 26 miles north of Key West. There are hundreds of islands in the Florida Keys chain and all are named so perhaps when the early settlers arrived at this island they had run out of appellations and merely called it No Name Key.

To get there turn off US 1 at Big Pine Key and drive west to the big modern bridge that leads to No Name Key. On the other side of the bridge the road suddenly narrows into little more than a trail and you can't help wondering why the bridge was ever built in the first place. The island has several side roads that are sandy and just waiting for the unwary driver so be careful if you leave the main road. As you approach the other side of the island you will see an abandoned house on the left and old derelict docks stretching out into the Gulf of Mexico. A path on your right leads through dense mangroves to where the rib bones of an old wooden ship lie partially submerged along the shoreline. Both sides of the paths through the mangrove swamp are excellent places to find old bottles and other relics of the past.

The shoreline along the Gulf side of No Name Key is a wonderful place to scrounge for driftwood of all sizes and shapes. Foundations of the houses of the early inhabitants dot the underbrush and cannonballs have been found in the interior of the island along with old stoves, parts of boats and dishes dating back to the early eighteen hundreds.

The central part of the island is covered with open forests of Caribbean Pine. If you visit the island in the evening just as it starts to turn dark and walk very quietly you are sure to see some of the wonderfully small Key deer coming out to graze in the open fields. These diminutive cousins of the northern white tails are on the increase due to strong protective measures by the conservation groups and No Name Key is one of the best places to view them.

The Florida Keys have been overdeveloped, dredged, devastated by hurricanes, trailer parked and tourist trapped until there is little of the tropical charm of the early years for the traveler to enjoy today. No Name Key lies like an undisturbed jewel for the modern day explorer. But you had better hurry — developers are now laying out the streets for a future sub-division.

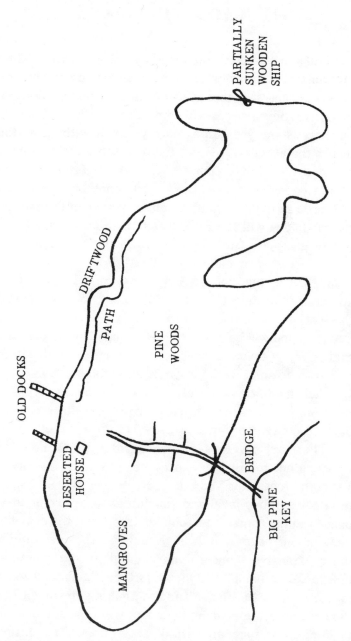

WITHLACOOCHEE CAVES

Did you ever have the urge to explore a cave? There is something mysterious and fascinating about underground caverns that awakens an adventurous spark in all of us. There are several commercial caves in Florida, but here is one you can explore yourself without getting lost in the process. It is located between Brooksville and Inverness in Citrus County. Start at the intersection of State Roads 480 and 491. Drive north on 491 for about one half mile passing a small ranch on your right. Just past the ranch you will see a small road with mailboxes on the left. Right across the highway from the mailboxes you will see a dirt trail leading to the east. Follow this trail for about half a mile and you will come to a large clearing surrounded by huge oak trees. Park here and walk east to the foot of one of the largest trees. Be careful, because suddenly you will be at the edge of a huge hole 15 feet deep that is one of the entrances to the caverns. Don't let the kids run around without your guidance! Also, if the weather has been very wet the road leading to the caves may bog your car down, so drive in carefully. It is a perfect shady spot for a picnic near the cave entrance.

There are several holes leading down into the caves that are not too difficult to descend. Use tree roots as hand and foot holds and take a flashlight. At the bottom the floor is fairly level and you can explore two or three large rooms going from one to the other by crawling under stone ledges and through tunnels. The cave may be more extensive than is apparent but except for small holes leading back into blackness there is no way to get too far from any of the entrances. Looking up you can see the fissures bringing dripping water from the surface and forming flowstone and small stalagtites. Thoughtless explorers in the past have broken off those that are within

The whole family can enjoy these small caverns.

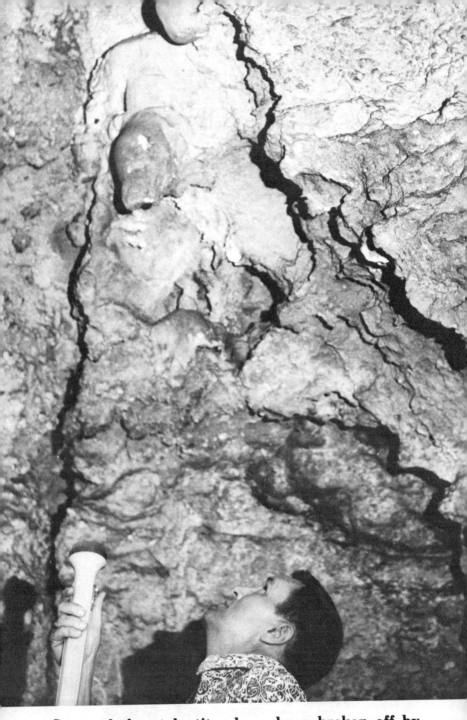

Some of the stalagtites have been broken off by souvenir hunters.

Oh, oh! Better not go any further!

easy reach but there are enough left so that you can see how nature is forming the beautiful stonework   above you.

Other caves are hidden away in the Withlacoochee State Forest in this area because this is typical cave country with rolling hills and numerous sinkholes where roofs of the underground caverns have fallen in to form deep pits and lakes. Local woodsmen and forestry workers can guide you to other caverns.

While in this area visit the firetower on top of Tillis Hill. After visiting the cave continue east on the dirt road to the second graded road and then turn north to the firetower sign. You are welcome to climb to the top of the tower and have a wonderful view of the interesting area surrounding the caves. Try to be there at sunset for a sight you will never forget.

Some of the Withlacoochee Caves have a narrow entrance. Who knows how far they lead . . . .

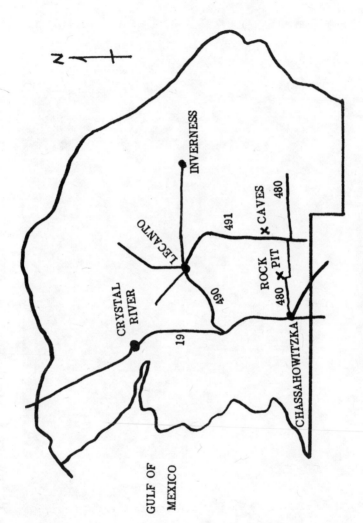

LOCATION OF CAVES IN CITRUS COUNTY

THE PINE CREST TRAIL

The state has officially named this narrow road SR 94, others call it the Loop road but I like the name Pinecrest trail. Not many people drive down this washboardy and dusty by-way for what is there; why use this hidden and little used trail when Hwy. 41 lies just to the north? For those who live there and other folks that have discovered its raw beauty the road means a way-of-life and a chance to live a little closer to nature and experience the rarity of solitude.

Drive west from the Palmetto Expressway on Hwy. 41, past the last remnants of civilization at Hwy. 27 and on into the vastness of the Everglades. A large sign on the left tells you that the 'glades lie ahead and to be careful because many animals cross the road. Many thousands of large and small creatures meet their deaths on this highway, but if you slow down for a raccoon some tourist in his sourball-8 will climb the backside of your car. You will pass the usual small businesses offering air boat rides, alligator wrestling and souvenirs and also pass hundreds of people fishing the bass-laden canal that borders the Tamiami Trail. You go past the huge pumping stations that keep the water at a proper level in the flats to the north and several 'authentic' Seminole Indian villages.

Miles and miles of six-foot-high sawgrass flats stretch away in every direction and in the distance you can see clumps of trees that are called hammocks after the Spanish word 'hamaca' meaning high, arable ground.

After you pass a restaurant and filling station on your right it is only a few miles to where the road turns to the northwest at forty mile bend. Take the road on your left to a small lake and wayside park. This is a good leg-stretching and picnicking spot before you continue on the slow gravel road ahead to Pinecrest. The best time to

enjoy this trail is on weekdays and not during the hunting
season when the road becomes well-used and hunters
actually camp with tents and pickup trucks on the right-
of-way.

You will cross many small bridges and find that if
you will take the time to stop at each one you will see
some of the beauty of nature that most people never take
the time to appreciate. Lean over the rail and look down
into the shallow water. Huge garfish lazily fin along
looking for crawfish and unlucky insects that fall into the
stream. Perhaps on the far bank a wild ibis will
noisily take off startling you with the beat of his six foot
wingspan. Bream, tadpoles and minnows are everywhere
and perhaps in the darkness under the bridge a big bass is
dozing. You are on the northern boundary of the
Everglades National Park and the sight of deer,
alligators and water moccasins is not uncommon.

Continuing on for about five miles brings you to the
hamlet of Pinecrest. Once a boom town in the 1920s,
Pinecrest is now sparsely settled and sleepy and gives
the visitor the impression that the residents are all
waiting for something to happen and probably wouldn't
care if something unusual did occur. I remember a few
years ago when we came into Pinecrest at eight o'clock
on a Sunday morning and watched two drunken indians
fighting with machetes in front of the local beer hall.
Later we saw them peacefully sleeping it off alongside
the dusty road and no one paid any attention to them.
Fishing, frogging, hunting and poaching are a way of life
in the Pinecrest area and there isn't a home without a
gun. You see, this is the **only inhabited area of mainland
Monroe County.** The nearest county law office is down in
the Keys a hundred miles away and the residents just
naturally tend to settle things in their own way and folks
don't look kindly on any antics by outsiders. Al Capone
lived here for awhile during prohibition, probably

because Pinecrest is just across the Dade County Line.

After you leave the town the road goes on for a couple of miles past scrub oak and weeds that hide the foundations of old homesites, a church and even a school house that once stood here. An oil well was drilled here years ago but was capped and abandoned after the oil flow was too small to turn a profit.

The road suddenly makes a sharp turn to the north. Drive on until you come to the first bridge at a wide spot in the road. I hope you are there as the sun goes down in the west because not only will you see a beautiful 'glades sunset, but you are now under the natural flyway the great birds use to return to their roosts for the night. Herons, egrets, anhingas and white ibis soar through the darkening sky to a rookery about one mile east of the trail. This area is one of the few remaining nesting places of the wood ibis, the only true American stork. They can be identified by their large blackish heads and black wingtips and are now classified as a rare and endangered species.

The road from here to Hwy. 41 leads beneath huge cypress and hardwoods with many streams and small bridges. If you feel like exploring and getting your feet wet, a walk through this primeval swamp is an unforgettable experience (be sure you have a compass!). Hunting shacks are tucked away beneath the trees, and game and swamp buggy trails crisscross the swamplands. Turkey buzzards sit hunched in the tops of dead pine trees and Spanish moss swinging from cypress limbs gives an eerie touch to this never-never land. Thousands of bromeliad plants adorn the tree trunks and rare orchids bloom in unseen beauty. As you reach the end of Pinecrest trail at the 'hard road' you will see hundreds of swamp buggies parked in a huge fenced yard waiting for the hunters who will awaken the noisy motors and turn the great turf-chewing wheels at the start of another hunting season. Somehow you wish the gates could be kept locked and that the home of the egret could be left undisturbed for all time.

PAYNES PRAIRIE

Just south of Gainesville you may cross a little-known but interesting aspect of Florida's geological history. If you are heading north to Gainesville leave I-75 at the Micanopy exit and drive one mile east to Hwy. 441 and then north for about four miles. At this point you will be descending from the hill country and suddenly you are greeted by a vast prairie extending to the hills of Gainesville in the distance. There is a rustic sign on the right side of the highway explaining the vista before you and this is a good stopping place to stretch your legs and take in the view.

Paynes Prairie extends three miles north to south and about eight miles east to west. At the present time it is a semi-dry marsh but at one time during the 1800s it was a shallow lake. Old-timers in the area claim that small steamboats carried goods from one side of the lake to the other and when the lake suddenly went dry the boats were marooned on the west side of the lake bottom. A hunter from Hawthorne claims to have seen the ribs of the old ships sticking up through the marsh grass.

At certain seasons of the year insect hatchings swarm across the highway at night and they all but blind motorists by smearing windshields with their bodies. At other times thousands of small frogs migrate across the road and create slippery road conditions.

The prairie has now been designated as a refuge for waterfowl and wildlife and will be preserved for future generations.

A new path opened by oil company exploration crews near the Pinecrest trail.

A storm brews over lonesome Paynes Prairie.

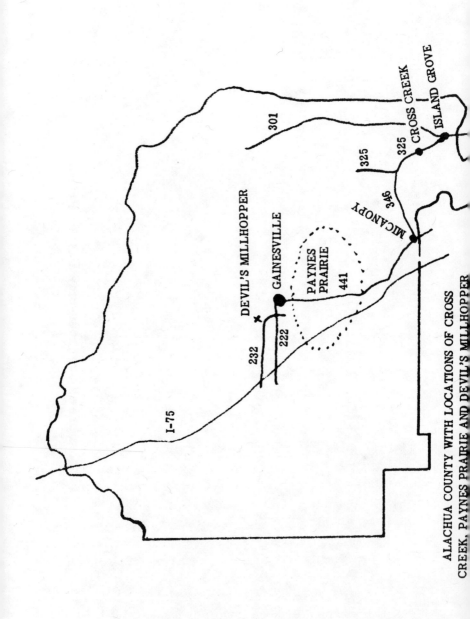

ALACHUA COUNTY WITH LOCATIONS OF CROSS
CREEK, PAYNES PRAIRIE AND DEVIL'S MILLHOPPER

CROSS CREEK

Southeast of Gainesville and only a few miles from Paynes Prairie one may explore the area around Cross Creek made famous by the writings of Marjorie Kinnan Rawlings. Here you may savor the nostalgia of a Florida that is fast fading away and soon may be seen no more. The unhurried shuffle of an old black woman with long cane poles over her shoulder as she makes her way to the edge of the creek to get her supper of tender catfish. The soft waving of spanish moss gracing the huge oaks that shade a hound dog asleep in the middle of the little traveled road. The quietness is broken only by the cry of a jaybird pestering a chattering squirrel while in the distance there is the paintive who-who of the mourning dove, the gay song of the mother quail or perhaps the long drawn out siren of a cicada.

Cross Creek has changed, of course, since Mrs. Rawlings lived there and wrote her book of that name, but enough of the old remains to make your visit worthwhile. Go to the intersection of State Rd. 325 and U.S. 301 in Alachua County and then drive west on 325 for four miles to Cross Creek which flows south from Lake Lochloosa. On the way you will pass Mrs. Rawlings' old homestead which is well marked with a roadside sign. To really enjoy your visit try to be there early on a weekday morning. Park near her homestead and walk the quiet road down to the river. The people you will meet will say 'howdy' and will take the time to chat a spell for there is no reason to hurry. The view from the bridge over Cross Creek is one of the most beautiful scenes in Florida.

By the time you get back to your car someone will have opened the house for the day and you can browse through the rooms described in so much detail by Mrs. Rawlings. Besides 'Cross Creek', she wrote 'South Moon

Fishing is a way of life between the lakes at Cross Creek.

Looking north from the bridge that spans Cross Creek.

Under', 'Golden Apples' and the Pulitzer Prize winning book 'The Yearling'. Mrs. Rawlings died in 1953 and willed her orange groves and old home to the people of Florida so that today we too may share what she loved so much.

Just south of her homestead is a large park on the edge of the river with picnic tables and restrooms. An ideal place to have your picnic lunch after enjoying the side roads of Cross Creek.

THE WAKULLA VOLCANO

This is a site that the casual visitor cannot visit. This fascinating natural phenomenon is hidden deep in an almost impenetrable   jungle known as the Pinhook swamp on the border of Wakulla and Jefferson counties south of Tallahassee. A volcano? Probably not, but **something** is there that belches huge columns of smoke and has mystified viewers since the first pioneers came to Florida.

Early sailing ships used the smoke column as a landmark for guidance to the port of St. Marks. Over the years it has been written about in various newspapers and magazines. It is a rare sight to see the smoke these days, but as recently as 1971 three fishermen from Perry reported a new "eruption".

Several expeditions have been formed to seek out the source of the smoke but so far only four men claim to have visited the site. Judge Porter and James Kirkland of Crawfordville found a rocky knoll with a small crater while on a hunting trip in the late 1920's. About 1932 Wm Wyatt and Fred Wimpee hacked their way southeast from Hwy. 98 towards the Gulf and found rocks as "big as houses" strewn over a four mile area. Neither group actually saw the smoke issuing from the ground, but either location might have been the right one.

The smoke varies in density, color and size. It appears and disappears. It was thought to be extinct when the smoke stopped after an earthquake shook Charleston, S.C. in 1886, but the smoke appeared again several years later.

To find the source will not be easy. Miles of mosquito and snake infested swamp must be penetrated. Much of the area cannot be walked but must be waded with a machete clearing every foot of the way. Jeep trails cross through some of the jungle, however it is a wildlife management area and various restrictions apply to the use of guns, camping and fires.

If you talk to nearby residents you will get conflicting stories and theories; that the whole story is a myth and the smoke never existed; that it was a Civil War slave camp and hasn't been in operation for over a hundred years; that it is a natural gas well ignited by lightning and extinguished by high tides; that it is a hot spring and the "smoke" is steam. Whatever the explanation, the true origin has not been proven and the site has not been visited, photographed or investigated scientifically. Someday I hope to penetrate that jungle myself. . . .

Chockoloskee Island

Smallwood's old store and post office at Chockoloskee.

White herons are a common sight along Jane's Highway.

Marjorie Kinnan Rawlings' home.

Hanging Spanish moss accents the tranquillity of Cross Creek.

Sunset west of Cross Creek.

The remains of Duke Alexander's tomb in the abandoned cemetery near Kismet.

Sideroads are calling you to explore the Ocala Forest.

An old engine now sleeps at Gulf Hammock.

Steinhatchee Falls

Steinhatchee Village and docks.

Old Quarry near Chassalowitzka.

Trail leading to the Withlacoochee Caves.

Stumps of ancient Cypress trees left by the loggers near Copeland.

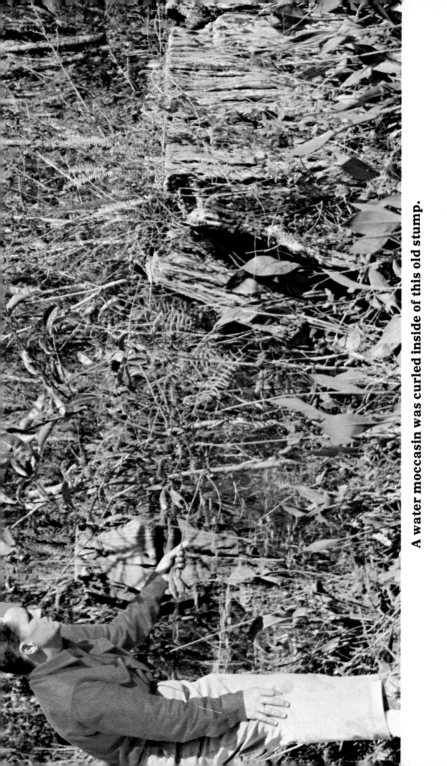

A water moccasin was curled inside of this old stump.

The dredge that built part of the Tamiami Trail.

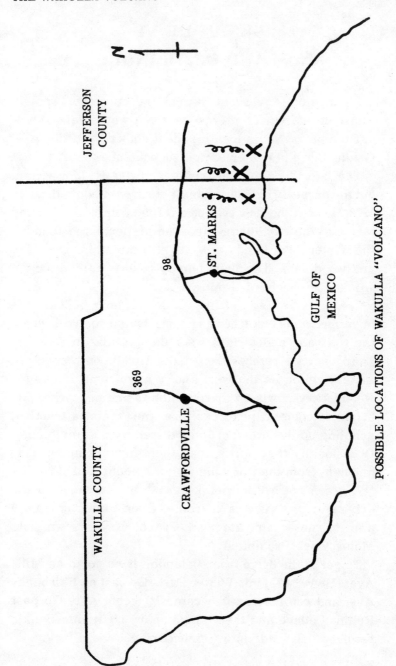

POSSIBLE LOCATIONS OF WAKULLA "VOLCANO"

GENIUS DRIVE —
AN ISLAND OF TRANQUILITY

I think almost everyone likes to find "tuckaway spots". Those little areas of interest that you would never know existed unless some local resident showed you the way. Genius Drive in Winter Park is such a place.

The late Chicago industrialist Charles H. Morris laid out the property in 1920 and built his dream home there in 1938. He kept the 150 acres as a refuge from the noise and bustle of the city surrounding the property and founded the Winter Park Land Co. which still maintains the drive and woodlands. The short bumpy road is named for the wife of Dr. Richard Genius.

Traffic is limited to fifteen miles an hour beneath the huge spreading oak trees as peacocks and squirrels cross the road and pedestrians walk thoughtfully in solitude. The property stretches from Lake Mizelle on the east to Lake Virginia on the west and is a welcome haven for woodpeckers, owls, mallards, rabbits and peacocks. The brightly colored peacocks are the main attraction, gobbling up the bread crumbs tossed by passing hikers. Occasionally they will spread their fans, bringing oohs and aahs from the watching visitors, young and old alike.

A green and white metal sign at the entrance to the drive states: "Visitors welcome. Open to public from 9 a.m. to sunset. Private road. Travel at your own risk. Motorcycles Prohibited."

To get to the drive from Orlando, drive north on Mills Ave. (Hwy. 17-92) into Winter Park. Go east on Fairbanks Ave. and continue as it becomes Osceola Ave. Go past Rollins College and then take a sharp right onto Henkle Circle which leads into Genius Drive.

A SPIRITUAL VISIT

Forty miles east of Orlando and seven miles west of DeLand is a small village of 400 residents. . . a relic of the past and a stepping stone to the future. This is Cassadaga. Thousands of visitors come to this out of the way hamlet every winter for spiritual help, worship, consultation with mediums, possible communication with their dead loved ones and just plain curiosity.

Cassadaga was founded in the 1880's by George Colby. He was led to this particular spot by messages from the spirit world and here he built his church and started the town that is now known all over the world as a center for the Spiritualist movement. The church now holds services every Sunday afternoon at 2:30 for worship, healing and communication with the dead. You do not have to be a member of the faith to attend as all are welcome. Some come as skeptics and then leave with more open minds, realizing that they may have been too quick to judge others because they were different.

The town itself is interesting. Winding bumpy roads take you past old houses built at the turn of the century. Wire and stone fences that were built for protection against packs of wild dogs still surround the homes that are comfortably nestled beneath huge spreading oak trees. A small lake behind the church supports a flock of ducks, framed by the gently draperies of spanish moss hanging from the old trees. A bronze plaque in front of the church was erected to the memory of Mr. Colby and describes how he was led to this spot by the spirits.

Each year more and more people are coming to Cassadaga to try and find answers to life's mysteries and many leave with a new awareness of the Spiritualist faith and teachings.

IN MEMORY OF
GEORGE P. COLBY
JANUARY 6, 1848   JULY 27, 1933
PIKE, N.Y.   CASSADAGA, FLORIDA

HE CAME TO FLORIDA IN 1875 AND WAS LEAD
THROUGH THE WILDERNESS BY HIS SPIRIT GUIDES
"SENECA," "THE PHILOSOPHER" AND "THE UNKNOWN"
TO THE PRESENT LOCATION OF THE SOUTHERN
CASSADAGA SPIRITUALIST ASSOCIATION.

THEY INSTRUCTED HIM TO ORGANIZE A
PSYCHIC CENTER. ON THIS SITE HE PREEMPTED A CLAIM
IN 1889 AND DONATED 35 ACRES OF LAND IN 1895.
THE PERMANENT ORGANIZATION WAS COMPLETED IN
1895. THIS WAS THE FULFILLMENT OF A PROPHECY
MADE WHEN A CHILD THAT HE WOULD ESTABLISH A
SPIRITUALIST CENTER IN THE SOUTH.

HIS PSYCHIC WORK EXTENDED
OVER A PERIOD OF 75 YEARS.
HIS WATCHWORD "TRANQUILIDAD"

FEDERATED CASSADAGA WOMAN'S CLUB   ERECTED 1947

Plaque erected in George Colley's memory.

The First Spiritualist Church.

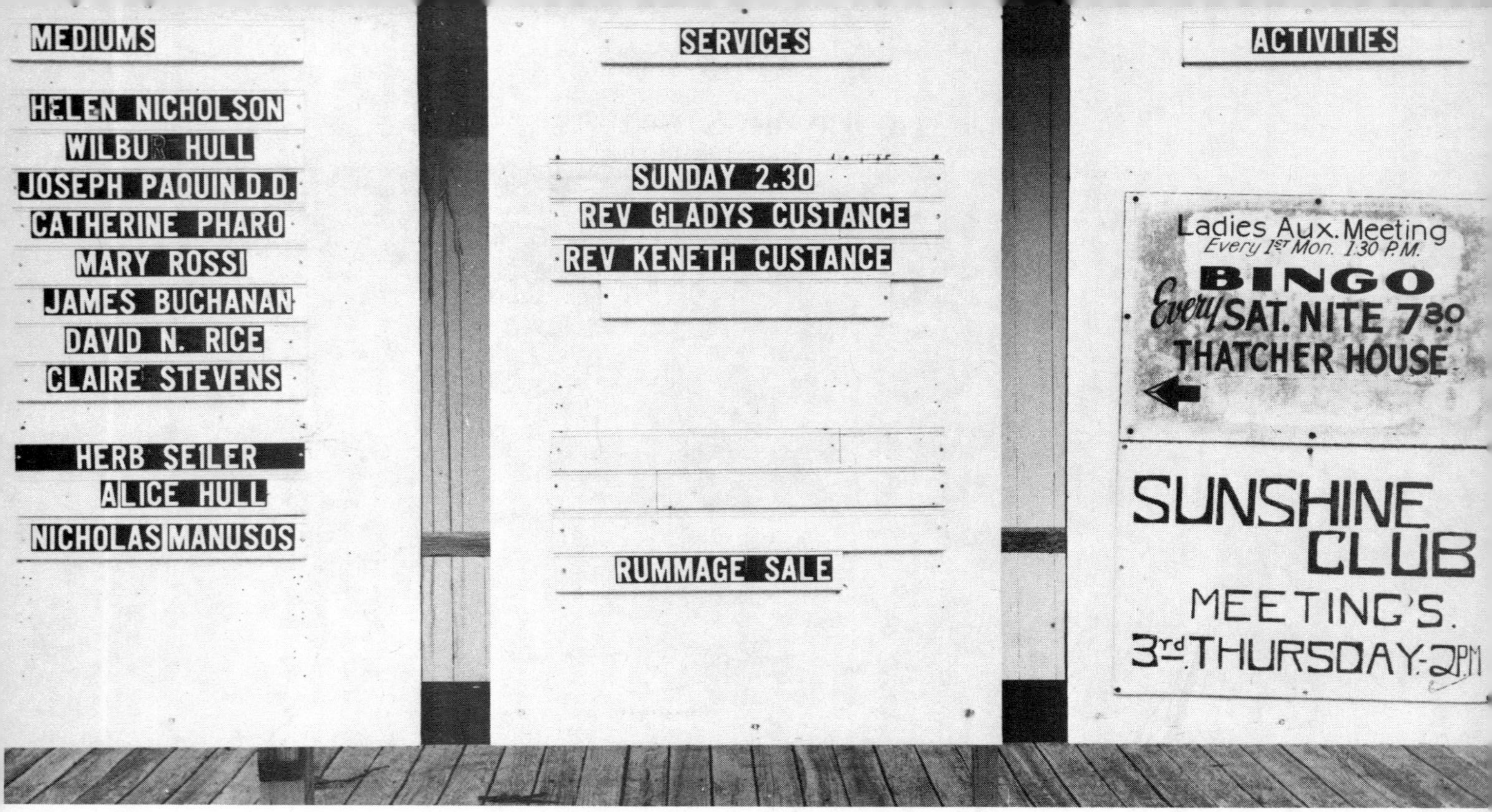

ACTIVITIES

Ladies Aux. Meeting
Every 1st Mon. 1:30 P.M.

BINGO
Every SAT. NITE 7:30
THATCHER HOUSE

SUNSHINE CLUB
MEETING'S
3rd THURSDAY: 2 PM

SERVICES

SUNDAY 2:30
REV GLADYS CUSTANCE
REV KENETH CUSTANCE

RUMMAGE SALE

MEDIUMS

HELEN NICHOLSON
WILBUR HULL
JOSEPH PAQUIN D.D.
CATHERINE PHARO
MARY ROSSI
JAMES BUCHANAN
DAVID N. RICE
CLAIRE STEVENS

HERB SEILER
ALICE HULL
NICHOLAS MANUSOS

Something for everyone at Cassadega.

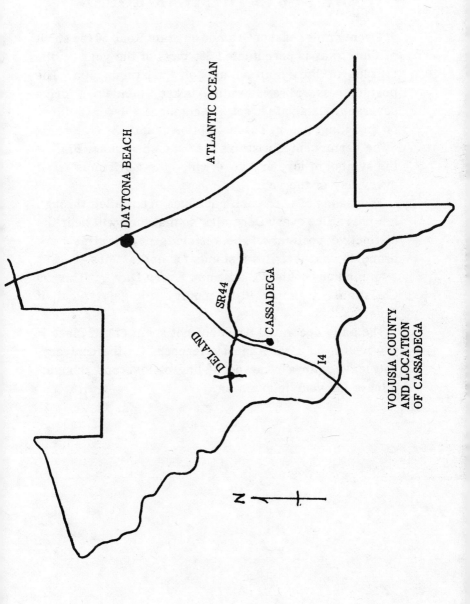

ATLANTIC OCEAN

DAYTONA BEACH

SR44

CASSADEGA

DELAND

I4

VOLUSIA COUNTY
AND LOCATION
OF CASSADEGA

N

CHRISTMAS THE YEAR ROUND

Twenty miles east of Orlando on State Road 50 the spirit of Christmas is perpetuated 365 days of the year by the citizens of the small village of Christmas, Fla. The postmistress, Miss Juanita Tucker, headed a drive several years ago to erect a permanently decorated tree on the village green. The inscription next to the tree reads "The permanent Christmas tree at Christmas, Fla., is the symbol of love and good will -- the Christmas spirit every day of the year."

Thousands of cards and packages are mailed through her post office every December so that they will bear the distinctive postmark. The residents of Christmas are proud of what their town stands for and as Mrs. Tucker wrote in her booklet "Christmas Every Day", "This is Christmas, a simple little country village, typical of America."

The gaily decorated tree does not seem out of place if you visit it on a hot August afternoon. On the contrary, you leave with a renewed feeling of love and thoughtfulness for your fellow man.

TO GET AWAY FROM IT ALL

Speed, noise, neon, turnpikes, tourist traps, commercialism, crowds and the feeling of being pushed down the tourist trail along with thousands of others who came to see Florida and don't know where to find it. It doesn't have to be that way. Let's take a few side roads and discover the tranquility you may be seeking. Along the way you will be near all the famous attractions Florida has to offer and of course you may want to visit many of them, but my purpose here is to lead you to the fascintating and lonely by-ways.

Driving south from Tallahassee takes you through some of the most beautiful pine forests in the state. **Wakula County** is laced with well graded gravel roads that lead to little known spots such as Arran and Spring Creek. Here Florida was touched by the civil war at the ^attle of Natural Bridge and the area was one of the first to be settled in the early 1800's.

Taking Hwy. 98 through Perry turn right on State Road 51. A few miles down this road you will see a sign on the left for **Steinhatchee Falls.** This is a beautiful little picknicking or camping site that is being preserved in a primitive state. Overlooking the Steinhatchee falls, the grounds are clean, restful and unbelievably quiet except for the murmur of the falling water. Trails lead off along the banks of the river where quiet pools can be found that offer fine black bass fishing. Raccoons are numerous at night and will steal quietly away with any food that is carelessly left on your table. Deer are numerous and you will probably see them if you watch carefully along the road at night.

Further on down SR 51 lies the little fishing village of **Steinhatchee.** The rather remote location of this town makes it an appealing retreat for those who love the sea

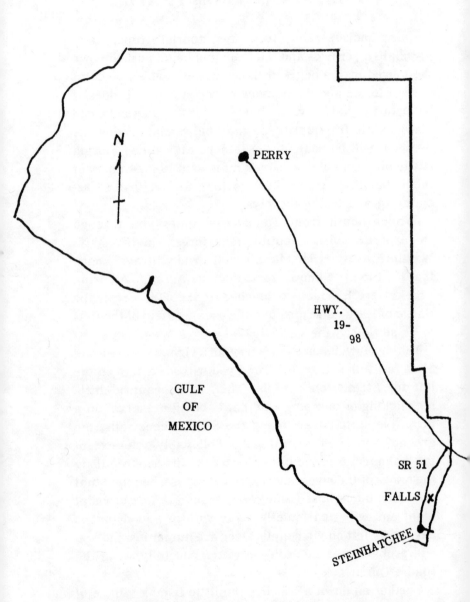

TAYLOR COUNTY SHOWING STEINHATCHEE AND FALLS

and fishing. Fish camps, motels and small restaurants line the edge of the mouth of the river. There is quiet here except for the murmur of fishing boats heading out into the Gulf and the cries of the seagulls feeding on the flats at low tide. One of the special mouth watering treats along this section of the coast is smoked mullet. Be sure to try some before you leave.

To return to Hwy. 98, cross the rickety wooden bridge to the south side of the river and drive about five miles east to the main highway. Heading south you will cross the historic Suwanee River and then pass through a wide spot in the road called **Gulf Hammock.** On the west side of the highway there is an old logging railroad engine preserved by the state for future generations so that the age of steam engines would not be forgotten. The kids (and adults, too!) can clamber all over this relic which makes a good background for snapshots.

At this point you can head east to see Cross Creek and Paines Prairie as described in previous chapters or you can continue on to the **Withlacoochee Cave area.** At Chassahowitzka on Hwy. 98, take SR 480 east which winds through rolling hills for several miles and then abruptly stops at an intersection of two small dirt roads. Either one will bring you out to the black top again in about a mile, but take the one that goes straight ahead. After a few blocks, you will see huge stones on the left that surround one of the deepest holes in Florida. This is an abandoned quarry about 100 feet deep, rimmed by large oak trees with a dry and rocky bottom that fairly buzzes with rattlesnakes. The pit is on private property and permission should be obtained before crossing the fence. You are now only about a mile from the Withlacoochee caves described in an earlier chapter.

Further down the coast you might want to see the largest camphor tree in the world at **Zephyrhills.** Camphor is not produced commercially in this country but is

imported from Formosa so this tree was probably
planted as an ornamental many years ago and has now
reached a stupendous size. To see it, start at the intersection of 5th Ave. and 12th St. in Zephyrhills and go
north on 12th (Wire Road) for 2.8 miles to SR 530 and then
go east for two miles. You will see the tree on the left in
the front yard of a private home. You may take pictures,
of course, but please do not bother the owners.

The Tampa-St. Petersburg area offers many commercial attractions but there is also one spot that to me is
one of the most fascinating areas you can explore.
Egmont Key lies at the entrance to Tampa Bay and was
used for a hundred years as the major defensive fort for
the harbor and the inland settlements. The old gun emplacements from the Civil War, the ruins of the soldier's
barracks, the brick roads, the remains of a short railroad
and the weed hidden relics of the past are there for you to
see and explore. Except for a small Coast Guard station
on one end of the island, it is deserted. You can feel
history around you on every side as you wander through
the ruins of our war torn past. Egmont Key is reached by
boat only. You can use your own, of course, or rent one
from one of the nearby marinas. There is no water or gas
available on the island, so be sure to come well prepared.

Bradenton lies on the south side of the bay. In 1843 Dr.
Joseph Braden settled here and carved an 1100 acre sugar
plantation. Besides building a sugar mill, he erected a
two and a half story castle with eight rooms, large halls
and eight fireplaces. The walls were constructed from
"tabby" which is a combination of lime, sand, crushed
shells and water moulded together into large bricks.
Slave labor was used in the construction and when
finished, the castle was a refuge and fort for the nearby
settlers during indian attacks. A forest fire in 1903
destroyed everything but the walls which remain today
as a mute reminder of Florida's pioneer history. You can

Sharks teeth and other fossils recovered from the Peace River at Arcadia.

see the ruins in east Bradenton at the intersection of Plaza St. and Braden Castle Drive.

A giant step backward in time awaits you 38 miles southeast of Bradenton at **Arcadia.** At one time in Florida's geological history the Peace River was part of the coastline when most of south Florida was under the seas. Today you can search the west bank and shallows of the river just south of Arcadia bridge and find numerous fossils, bones and shark's teeth protruding from the mud and sand. Specific finds in the past have included mastodon bones, teeth from a giant sloth, shark's teeth eight inches long and a turtle shell nine feet long. Specimens sent to the Smithsonian Institution were dated as being a part of the late Miocene era which ended twelve million years ago.

If you drive south from Arcadia on SR 31 you will cross the **Caloosahatchee River** which at one time was a main artery for river boats carrying goods to the interior. Looking west from the top of the bridge you will see the rotting hulks of some of these old craft resting in the shoals on the north side of the river. It is a rather rugged walk along the shore to reach the wrecks, but you might want to try it just because "they are there!"

South of the river and a little west are the Florida **oil fields.** Centered around Felda, these oil wells have been producing for many years. Not many people visiting Florida know that oil is becoming more and more economically important to the state. At the present time conservation forces are fighting to stop further exploration and drilling for oil in the Big Cypress Swamp further south, fearing that the wells and attendant construction would endanger one of the last strongholds of the dwindling Florida wildlife.

The fantastic Florida wildlife is all around you as you drive through the state but so few people have the time or means to get back into the swamps and pine woods to really enjoy the wilderness. Therefore we are going to break the rule of this book to only list those things that can be enjoyed free. The **Corkscrew Swamp Sanctuary** on State Road 846 twenty one miles east of U.S. 41 is the ideal place to get close to the wildlife of the Sunshine State. Admission is $2.00 with children under 12 free and if you love nature the price is worth every penny. In 1954 the Audubon Society saved the 10 square mile area from the lumber interests that were going to cut the last stand of virgin bald cypress in the state. They preserved the 700 year old trees and the surrounding wilderness so that you and I today can see a beautiful example of Florida's natural environment. A mile - long boardwalk winds through huge moss laden trees shading the abundant plant and animal life beneath. A self guided tour will show you alligators, snakes, fish and if you are lucky, the wood ibis. This huge bird is the only true American Stork and this sanctuary is the only nesting place left for them besides a small area south of the Tamiami Trail. Their black and ugly heads have earned for them the nickname of "ironhead" and they can be identified in flight by their large wings tipped with black. The early settlers and hunters found them to be delicious eating and nearly hunted them to extinction but today they are making a slow comeback through the efforts of the Audubon Society. If you have a group interested in seeing this wonderland, guided tours can be arranged in advance.

If you are going down into the Keys, and most Florida travelers eventually do, you might be interested in a little known aspect of early days mosquito control. Today the spray planes and fogging machines have made life more endurable for the Keys residents, but back in the twenties the sand gnats and mosquitos were thick and vicious. One old timer said you could swing a pint pail through the air and collect a quartful. In March of 1929, Mr. Perky of Sugarloaf Key erected a huge bat tower on his property to attract a bat population that hopefully would wipe out the pesky 'skeeters. The tower was built according to plans that were sent from Texas and was constructed with cypress shingles and huge 12 by 12 pine timbers. The Texas inventor then sent Mr. Perky a sealed box that contained a special bat attracting formula. This bait was placed in the tower and everyone waited for the swarms of bats to come to their new home. They are still waiting, as the bats never arrived and the tower stands today as a monument to one man's dream of controlling mosquitos. You may visit this curious structure behind the resort on Sugarloaf Key just off U.S. 1. Ask any local resident for directions.

To see the types of vegetation native to the Keys you can take a nature walk on **Islamorada.** The local chamber of commerce has a pamphlet describing the plants that are numbered along the walkway created by the C of C and the Izaak Walton League.

Key West has a large number of attractions, of course, and to get an idea of how Key West is laid out and what you might want to stop and see take the **Pelican Path route.** You pick up a pamphlet at the Old Island Restoration Foundation on Old Mallory Square and then follow the Pelican signs for a one and one half hour self guided tour that covers 32 points of interest.

As you drive over the Keys bridge you are being supported in many cases by the old railroad bed laid down by Henry Flagler back in the twenties. Destroyed by a devastating hurricane, the railroad was never rebuilt, but instead the present highway was constructed using the old railbed. On some of the bridges the railings were made from the old rails. Notice that huge pipe that follows the highway? That pipe supplies the only source of water for the long string of keys, the water being pumped from wells on the mainland. Key West has a new desalinization plant but the rest of the Keys depend on piped water.

Further up on the east coast at Coral Gables there is a very unusual monument. **Coral Gables** is a sister city of Cartagena, Columbia in the People to People program. To remind residents and visitors of their friendly ties with that South American country, a monument has been erected in Cartagena Plaza. It is a replica of a statue in Cartagena of a huge pair of old shoes called "Los Zapatos Viejos". Luis Carlos Lopez, a Columbian poet wrote fondly of his city and compared it to a comfortable pair of old shoes in his poem "A Mi Ciudad Nativa" and the statue was erected to commemorate his thoughts.

Miami is many things to many people and there is something there for everyone. There is a little known spot on the far north side that fairly reeks with history and hopefully will be preserved for future generations. The **natural bridge** is located at N.E. 135th St. and 16th Ave. on the north side of the intersection. Indians used the area as a gathering place hundreds and perhaps thousands of years ago as evidenced by the numerous pottery shards protruding from an indian mound a few yards east under a shading oak tree. The east side of the bridge was also the site of an early Spanish mission that flourished briefly in the 1600's. The narrow road crossing the bridge and leading off to the north is part of the old Dixie Highway, at one time the only road leading into the city from the north. During prohibition the natural bridge was a pick up point for bootleggers and rum runners. The remains of some of the stills can still be found deep in the mangroves bordering Arch Creek south of the bridge. Before World War II there were only woods and undergrowth surrounding the bridge where hunters roamed for deer, rabbits and bobcats. Today the apartments and stores are closing in on this last remnant of Miami's early and colorful history.

U.S. Hwy. 1 from Miami through West Palm Beach is so jammed with commercial attractions that there are

probably more things to see and do along that crowded
road than any place else in the United States. So be it.
There are a few quiet spots to relax and recuperate,
however, if you want a change from the glitter and
crowds. Try an out of the way corner in one of the
numerous city parks. Visit one of the many fine libraries.
Go the the beach. "The beach", you say? Isn't that one of
the crowded places we are trying to avoid for a change?
Not if you walk a little ways along the ocean shoreline.
The Florida courts have ruled that **all** of the beaches are
for the use of the public below the high tide mark. As long
as you stay close to the surf you can wander for miles
away from the crowded areas, beachcomb, swim, fish or
just lie on the sand. There are 1016 miles of **sand** beaches
and over 4,000 miles of actual coastline awaiting you.

Further north turn east off Hwy. 1 at Stuart and go over
the intracoastal waterway to the ocean. During the early
days of Florida's history, ships plying the Gulfstream
would pass close to the coastline to take advantage of the
prevailing currents, however in so doing they would run
afoul of the numerous reefs and sand bars. Wrecks were
so common that the government established **houses of
refuge** so that the stranded mariners would have food and
shelter. The only remaining lifesaving station of this sort
has been preserved on the beach at Stuart. A fascinating
museum of the sea and wrecks is open to the public along
with a turtle hatchery. If you are on the east coast of
Florida in June you can watch the giant sea turtles come
up out of the ocean at night to build their nests and lay
dozens of ping pong ball size eggs. Because the nesting
spots have been taken over by sea walls and hotels in so
many areas, many groups are trying to help the turtles by
establishing hatcheries and then releasing the young
when they are old enough to fend for themselves. Such a
hatchery has been built at the House of Refuge. Just north
of the museum is a very unusual stretch of coastline. The
ancient coral formations along the beach have been worn

away and now form many weird and unusual shapes. Small underwater caves have been hollowed out by the action of the waves until a part of the roof of the cave was worn through. During periods of high tide and large waves the seawater spouts through these blowholes like a wild fountain of nature. Many ships were wrecked along this beach and sometimes relics can be found after a storm has rearranged the sand.

Most museums in Florida charge an admission fee so it is refreshing to find the free **St. Lucie County Museum** at 414 Seaway Drive in Ft. Pierce. A Seminole Indian village, artifacts from Spanish galleons and many other items make this an interesting stop.

Kennedy Space Center at Cape Canaveral (yes, there still is a Cape Canaveral) has tours by bus that charge a fare, but did you know that you can tour the Center yourself without charge? Every Sunday you can drive through the gate near the Visitors Center south of Titusville and followed the signs for the Drive Yourself tour around the launching pads. There is another entry point at Gate 1 north of Cocoa Beach. The drive takes about 45 minutes so be sure you have enough gas as there are no filling stations along the way.

West of the Cape are the **central highlands** of Florida. Rolling hills, citrus groves and forests make driving through this country a real pleasure. The scenery is ever changing and is best viewed by taking the small county roads and graveled by-ways. Here you will not be harrassed by impatient drivers behind you and you can take your time to really enjoy the Florida between the coasts. For instance, here is a two hour drive through some of the most scenic spots in the state: Start at Winter Garden on the south side of Lake Apopka. Drive east on 437 to Plymouth and then north on 441 to Tavares and then southwest on 19 to Howey in the Hills where you pick up 455 to Montverde and Minneola. Drive on 27 to Clermont

where 50 will take you back to your starting point at
Winter Garden.

Excursions like this will give you the real "feel" of
central Florida. Make up your own from any part of the
state. The gas company maps only show the main routes
in most cases so the county maps available at court-
houses in every county seat are excellent for finding the
roads you want to explore. Many families just drive and
turn off at any small road and are delighted at the
unusual and scenic spots they find in out of the way
places. (A tip here. . . if you see a row of mailboxes at the
entrance to a small road this means that it is a dead end
and the road probably ends up in a farmer's front yard.)

If you are a horseman, the Ocala area offers you a
chance to visit some of the most famous **thoroughbred
breeding farms** in the nation. Go to the Ocala Chamber of
Commerce and they will give you free maps showing the
location of the farms and the hours they allow visitors.

Florida's unique geology has created many wonderful
formations such as the numerous lakes, springs and
caves. It is thought by scientists that the central part of
the state is undermined with many caverns that have
no opening to the upper world. When the roofs of these
caves wear through to the surface a sinkhole is formed
and, depending on the water conditions, either a lake is
born or there is a huge hole opened to the sky. The **Devil's
Millhopper** near Gainesville is a good example of this
geological activity. Long known to local residents, this
big sinkhole is a favorite picnic area and hours can be
spent exploring it's nooks and crannies. Small springs
cascade from the sides of the cliffs to form a creek that
then disappears into a hole in the bottom. Shark's teeth
and other fossils have been exposed by the formation of
this sinkhole and the geology of the upper crust of Florida
can be studied in the strata of the sides. To get there take
329 north from the west side of Gainesville, cross 222 and

continue on for one mile until the road makes a left turn to the west. The dirt road you see on the north side is the entrance to the Millhopper area.

A few miles north of Gainesville is **Fort White** on the Ithatockee River. This little town is the jumping off place for one of the most unusual sports in the world...tubing. The idea is that you rent a large innertube from one of the nearby filling stations, get into your bathing suit and then jump into the river for a floating tour of the beautiful Ithatockee River. Anyone in the area can fill you in on all the details. It offers a lot of family fun and is sure to make an interlude in your travels that will be talked of for years to come!

Back over on the east coast in **Titusville** is a house with a curious history. Back in 1881 an Italian nobleman, Eicole Tamajo, Duke of Castelellucia, bought the famed Dummitt Grove and married Jennie Anheuser of the Budweiser beer family. He built a two story mansion for her on Merritt Island and used for lumber wood salvaged from the wrecked sailing ship Santa Cruz. Planking on the outside was 30 feet long and the center posts for the two spiral staircases were the ship's masts. He built the house in an octagon shape, believing that this design would streamline the structure and prevent damage from hurricanes. After a domestic squabble he partitioned the old house into two parts, his and hers. The Duke finally went back to Italy and died in 1892. When NASA needed the land for the space program the old building was moved to a public park in Titusville where you can see it today.

Just west of US 1 near **New Smyrna Beach** are some ancient ruins that have a rather mysterious past. No one is quite sure if the old walls were built as a Spanish mission in the 1600's or by the British as a sugar mill. What is known for a fact is that it was being used as a sugar mill in the 1830's when the Indians burned it during the Seminole War. The thick walls were built from local coquina rock and although now overgrown with vines and trees, they are still strong and sturdy. Part of the sugar mill engine and a huge iron cooking kettle are all that remains of the mill itself. On the ocean side of New Smyrna Beach is the largest indian mound in the state. It is so high that the old sailing charts had it marked as an aid to navigation. You can find it at the south end of the beach highway where the road reaches the Cape Kennedy Air Force Station.

Everyone who visits **Daytona Beach** sooner or later wants to drive on the hard sands along the shore but I would like to throw in a word of caution. Salt spray on and under your car can eat away the finish like acid so be sure to hose your vehicle down with fresh water as soon as possible after any exposure. Also, be sure not to park too close to the water if the tide is rising. If you get stuck it will cost you a pretty penny for the tow truck.

If you are driving north to Jacksonville and have plenty of time there is an interesting side road you might like to travel. Starting at Palatka drive north for about 10 miles on Hwy. 17 to Bostwick. Take the gravel road heading northeast that parallels the railroad. After about six miles you will come to a bend in the road with two or three buildings and a gate on the right. This is the ghost town of **West Tocoi.** Back in the 1800's the railroad followed the east side of the St. Johns River and unloaded passengers and goods at the hamlet of East Tocoi. From there a ferry carried the people and freight across the river to West Tocoi where the Jacksonville, Tampa and Key West Railroad had a terminus. Although the town of West Tocoi is still shown on modern maps, there is nothing left but a few rotting pilings in the river bank and one or two deserted houses. (This all private land and posted).

Following this gravel road brings you to **Green Cove Springs,** the side of a Spanish fort erected in 1737 by St.

Francis DePupa. Destroyed by the British in 1740 the fort side earthworks are still visible. You can turn east at this point and cross the St. Johns River on Hwy. 16 to State Road 13 that borders the river all the way north to Jacksonville. You will drive through villages like Switzerland and Mandarin sleeping beneath giant oak trees and be able to take little trails to the river's edge for views of the river and some ideal picnic areas.

Heading west from Jacksonville takes you through the early **pioneer country** that was the first part of Florida to be settled. Almost every small town has buildings still standing that were built before the Seminole Wars and are still in use today. For instance, in Baker County there is the Brown house, constructed in 1833 as a small fortress for protection agains maurauding indians. The small roads leading to the house are interesting for other reasons, too. If you are from the north and have ever wondered where all your robins went in the winter, you will find all your feathered friends by the millions along the roads of Baker County during the winter months. Here, too, is a good place to spot a wild hog or bear, especially in the evening. From Interstate 10 get off at Sanderson and follow 127 north for twelve and a half miles where you will cross the middle prong of the St. Mary's River and see road 122 on the left a half a mile further on. Turn right at the next dirt road and drive for a half a mile to an intersection. Turn right, go ¼ of a mile and turn right again. The Brown house is another ¼ of a mile on your right.

After becoming lost and finding your way back you might want to go on to Bradford County and stop at the **strawberry** fields near Lawtey. During April and May the strawberries are ripe and many farms let you pick your own for a nominal price. In July and August the **tobacco auctions** are held throughout the northern part of the state with the largest and oldest located in Live Oak. Visitors are welcome.

If you are near Live Oak and feel like having a picnic and a refreshing swim, take Hwy. 51 southwest about 11 miles to Luraville. Go through the town and turn east at the Agricultural Inspection Station for about a half a block. Turn south and go about a mile to the end. You are now on a bluff overlooking the Suwanee River with Telford Spring at the base of the cliff to your right. There is good swimming, camping, and plenty of woods to explore all around you.

Traveling west toward the Tallahassee area there is a good leg stretching spot on the Suwanee River off Hwy. 90. This is the site of the ghost town of **Ellaville.** Former Gov. Drew had his mansion here before the Civil War and the old house was still standing until fire destroyed it a few years ago. There is a good park on the north side of the highway for picnics and fishing. A historical plaque tells of the history of long gone Ellaville.

The **panhandle of Florida** has many interesting things to see and do if you want to get away from the carnival areas like Panama Beach and the stench of the St. Joe paper mills. Hwy. 98 follows the Gulf of Mexico shoreline for miles through Franklin County and there are many places you can stop and beachcomb for shells, driftwood and perhaps artifacts from sunken ships.

In 1850 a Floridian by the name of Dr. John Gorrie invented the ice making machine and devised the first crude air conditioner. Near the watertower in Apalachicola the townspeople have built a small museum in his honor complete with a replica of his original machine. He really wasn't thinking of air conditioning as we know it, but merely wanted to devise a way to cool the victims of the fever that were under his care. Florida's summers are certainly more bearable because of his efforts!

One of the wildest and most primitive areas of Florida is known as Tates Hell. Located north and west of Carabelle, this swamp holds the answer to many tales of lost hunters who never returned, slave trading camps before the Civil War and hidden outlaw camps. Wildlife abounds in this dense cypress wilderness. Although owned for the most part by paper companies, the woods have not been extensively cut and offer the side road traveler a chance to see a semi-tropical forest. Drive north from Hwy. 98 on SR 65 at a point about five miles east of Eastpoint. From there go 16 miles north to Buck's Siding and drive east on a well graded road through the heart of the swamp. You will emerge after 18 miles at the Carrabelle airstrip near Hwy. 98.

Up near the Georgia border about six miles north of Bonifay on SR 177A is a place called Cracker City. This is a large tabernacle famous through the southeast for the Sunday evening Gospel singing and everyone is welcome to join with them as they make a "joyful noise unto the Lord". A local radio station broadcasts the program.

Away over in the tip of the panhandle there are some of the most beautiful beaches in the world along the Gulf of Mexico in Okaloosa County. Pure white sand dunes have been windcarved into flowing draperies that frame the blues and greens of the sea at their feet. You can park almost anywhere along the beach and let the whole family have a glorious time playing in the clean sand hills. A small campfire with a pan of fresh caught fish, a pot of coffee and a glorious sunset over the Gulf would make a fitting end to your ramblings over the side roads of Florida.

THE MOST INTERESTING ROADS?

From time to time, knowing that I have traveled Florida from one end to the other, folks have asked me what I thought were the most interesting roads in the state. I don't think that anyone has been on **every** road. That kind of a trip would take a lifetime. There are some, of course, that stick out in my memory, that I have a fond feeling for and try to travel on when in that area. These roads may not be to your liking or tastes, but thank goodness we are all different. Here are my favorites and I think you might enjoy them, too.

From Punta Rassa, the bridge and drive through Sanibel Island.

The Sunshine Skyway over Tampa Bay.

SR 491 from Hwy. 50 to Hwy. 98 just west of Brooksville.

Hwy. 42 from Altoona to Wiersdale.

The Seven Mile bridge on the way to Key West.

SR 13 from Jacksonville south to Hwy. 27.

SR 255 northwest of Mayo from Lee to Day.

Hwy. 98 from Carabelle to Medart.

Hwy. 441 from Zellwood to Mount Dora.

The peavine trail south from Kenansville to Hwy. 60.

SR 27 from Homestead to Flamingo.